Down the Rabbit Hole of Leadership

Manfred F. R. Kets de Vries

Down the Rabbit Hole of Leadership

Leadership Pathology in Everyday Life

palgrave
macmillan

Manfred F. R. Kets de Vries
INSEAD
Fontainebleau, France

ISBN 978-3-319-92461-8   ISBN 978-3-319-92462-5   (eBook)
https://doi.org/10.1007/978-3-319-92462-5

Library of Congress Control Number: 2018953037

This Palgrave Macmillan imprint is published by the registered company Springer Nature Switzerland AG
The registered company address is: Gewerbestrasse 11, 6330 Cham, Switzerland

Once, I overheard someone saying that experiencing gratitude and not expressing it is like buying a present and not giving it. With this in mind, I would like to dedicate this book to two women who have been very important to me for most of my working life. The first is Sheila Loxham, my long-time personal assistant, who has been a remarkable support to me over the years. I have always greatly appreciated her ability to reframe difficult situations in a very positive way. In that respect, she often plays the role of the counselor's counselor. The second person to whom I would like to express my gratitude (and with whom I have also worked for a very long time) is Elizabeth Florent-Treacy, senior lecturer at INSEAD, whose intellectual curiosity and creativity have always been a tremendous source of support to me.

The Palgrave Kets de Vries Library

Manfred F. R. Kets de Vries, Distinguished Professor of Leadership and Development and Organizational Change at INSEAD, is one of the world's leading thinkers on leadership, coaching, and the application of clinical psychology to individual and organizational change. Palgrave's professional business list operates at the interface between academic rigor and real-world implementation. Professor Kets de Vries's work exemplifies that perfect combination of intellectual depth and practical application and Palgrave is proud to bring almost a decade's worth of work together in the Palgrave Kets de Vries Library.

Sex, Money, Happiness, and Death
The Coaching Kaleidoscope[1]
Mindful Leadership Coaching
Coach and Couch (2nd edition)[2]
You Will Meet a Tall, Dark Stranger
Telling Fairy Tales in the Boardroom
Riding the Leadership Rollercoaster
Down the Rabbit Hole of Leadership

---

[1] Edited by Manfred F. R. Kets de Vries, Laura Guillén, Konstantin Korotov, Elizabeth Florent-Treacy.
[2] Edited by Manfred Kets de Vries, Konstantin Korotov, Elizabeth Florent-Treacy, Caroline Rook.

Contents

About the Author

Manfred F. R. Kets de Vries brings a different view to the much-studied subjects of leadership and the psychodynamics of individual and organizational change. Bringing to bear his knowledge and experience of economics (Econ. Drs., University of Amsterdam), management (ITP, MBA, and DBA, Harvard Business School), and psychoanalysis (Membership Canadian Psychoanalytic Society, Paris Psychoanalytic Society, and the International Psychoanalytic Association), Kets de Vries explores the interface between management theory, psychoanalysis, psychotherapy, executive coaching, and evolutionary psychology. His specific areas of interest are leadership (the bright and dark side), career dynamics, talent management, entrepreneurship, family business, cross-cultural management, succession planning, stress, C-suite team-building, executive coaching, change management, organizational design, management consulting, and organizational development.

The Distinguished Clinical Professor of Leadership Development and Organizational Change at INSEAD, Kets de Vries was the founding director of INSEAD's Global Leadership Centre. In addition, he is Programme Director of INSEAD's top management programme, The Challenge of Leadership: Creating Reflective Leaders, and the founder of the Executive Master Programme Consulting and Coaching for Change (and has received INSEAD's distinguished teacher award six times). He has also held professorships at McGill University, the École des Hautes Études Commerciales, Montreal, the European School for Management and Technology (ESMT), Berlin, and the Harvard Business School, and he has lectured at management institutions around the world. *The Financial Times, Le Capital, Wirtschaftswoche*, and *The Economist* have rated Manfred Kets de Vries among the world's leading management thinkers and among the most influential contributors to human resource management.

Kets de Vries is the author, co-author, or editor of 49 books, including *The Neurotic Organization*; *Leaders, Fools and Impostors*; *Life and Death in the Executive Fast Lane*; *The Leadership Mystique*; *The Happiness Equation*; *Are Leaders Born or Are They Made?: The Case of Alexander the Great*; *The New Russian Business Elite*; *Leadership by Terror*; *The Global Executive Leadership Inventory*; *The Leader on the Couch*; *Coach and Couch*; *Tricky Coaching*; *The Family Business on the Couch*; *Sex, Money, Happiness, and Death: The Quest for Authenticity*; *Reflections on Character and Leadership*; *Reflections on Leadership and Career Development*; *Reflections on Groups and Organizations*; *The Coaching Kaleidoscope*; *The Hedgehog Effect: The Secrets of Building High-Performance Teams*; *Mindful Leadership Coaching: Journeys into the Interior*; *You Will Meet a Tall Dark Stranger: Executive Coaching Challenges*; *Telling Fairy Tales in the Boardroom: How to Make Sure Your Organization Lives Happily Ever After*; and *Riding the Leadership Roller Coaster: An Observer's Guide*.

In addition, Kets de Vries has published more than 400 academic papers as chapters in books and as articles. He has also written approximately 100 case studies, including seven that received the Best Case of the Year award. He is a regular contributor to a number of magazines. His work has been featured in such publications as *The New York Times, The Wall Street Journal*, the *Los Angeles Times, Fortune, Businessweek, The Economist*, the *Financial Times*, and the *Harvard Business Review*. His books and articles have been translated into 31 languages. He writes regular blogs for *INSEAD Knowledge*, the *Harvard Business Review*, and *Het Financieele Dagblad*. He is a member of 17 editorial boards and has been elected a Fellow of the Academy of Management. He is a founding member of the International Society for the Psychoanalytic Study of Organizations (ISPSO), which has honored him as a lifetime member. Kets de Vries is also the first non-American recipient of the International Leadership Association Lifetime Achievement Award for his contributions to leadership research and development (he is considered one of the world's founding professionals in the development of leadership as a field and discipline). In addition, he received a Lifetime Achievement Award from Germany for his advancement of executive education. The American Psychological Association has honored him with the Harry and Miriam Levinson Award for his contributions to Organizational Consultation. He is the recipient of the Freud Memorial Award for his work to further the interface between management and psychoanalysis and has received the Vision of Excellence Award from the Harvard Institute of Coaching. Kets de Vries is also the first beneficiary of the INSEAD Dominique Héau Award for Inspiring Educational Excellence and the recipient of two honorary doctorates.

Kets de Vries works as a consultant on organizational design/transformation and strategic human resource management for leading US, Canadian, European, African, and Asian companies. As a global consultant in executive leadership development his clients have included ABB, ABN-AMRO, Aegon, Air Liquide, Alcan, Alcatel, Accenture, ATIC, Bain Consulting, Bang & Olufsen, Bonnier, BP, Cairn, Deutsche Bank, DMGT, Ericsson, GE Capital, Goldman Sachs, Heineken, Hudson, HypoVereinsbank, Investec, KPMG, Lego, Liberty Life, Lufthansa, Lundbeck, McKinsey, National Australian Bank, Nokia, Novartis, Novo Nordisk, Origin, SABMiller, Shell, SHV, Spencer Stuart, Standard Bank of South Africa, Unilever and Volvo Car Corporation. As an educator and consultant he has worked in more than 40 countries. In his role as a consultant, he is also the chair of the Kets de Vries Institute (KDVI), a boutique leadership development consulting organization.

The Dutch government has made Manfred Kets de Vries an Officer in the Order of Oranje Nassau. He was the first fly fisherman in Outer Mongolia and is a member of New York's Explorers Club. In his spare time he can be found in the rainforests or savannas of Central and Southern Africa, the Siberian taiga, the Ussuri krai, Kamchatka, the Pamir and Altai Mountains, Arnhemland, or within the Arctic Circle.

Part I

1

Introduction

*The rabbit hole went straight on like a tunnel for some way, and then dipped
suddenly down, so suddenly that Alice had not a moment to think about
stopping herself before she found herself falling down a very deep well. Either
the well was very deep, or she fell very slowly, for she had plenty of time as she
went down to look about her and to wonder what was going to happen next.*
—Lewis Carroll
*A philosopher is a blind man in a dark room looking for a black cat that isn't
there. A theologian is the man who finds it.*
—Unattributed. Collected by H. L. Mencken (*1942*)

In Lewis Carroll's novel *Alice's Adventures in Wonderland*, Alice is lazing in
the grass on a warm summer's day when she sees a White Rabbit hurrying
past, wearing a waistcoat and consulting his pocket watch. Intrigued, she
follows the rabbit and falls down a long burrow. She finds herself in a
strange and surreal place called Wonderland, where she encounters mys-
terious talking animals (including a hookah-smoking caterpillar), magical food, and a delusional royal court. One of the stranger creatures Alice
encounters during her adventures is the grinning Cheshire cat that can
appear and disappear at will, leaving only its smile behind. On the cat's
advice, Alice visits the March Hare, who spends his days at a never-ending

© The Author(s) 2019
M. F. R. Kets de Vries, *Down the Rabbit Hole of Leadership*,
https://doi.org/10.1007/978-3-319-92462-5_1

tea party with a Dormouse and a Mad Hatter. Eventually, she meets the Queen of Hearts, the mad tyrant who rules Wonderland. At the end of the story, the Knave of Hearts (one of the Queen of Hearts' guards) is charged with stealing some tarts. A trial is held and Alice is called as a witness. She ridicules the trial and the furious Queen orders "Off with her head!" Alice dismisses the entire court as "nothing but a pack of cards" and wakes up to realise she has been dreaming.

Alice's Adventures in Wonderland has been a much-loved novel since its publication in 1865, its fantasy and nonsense popular with children and adults alike. However, there is more to the story than we might initially think. Falling down the rabbit hole can be interpreted as a metaphor for entry into the unknown. The events that occur in the story correlate with the steps in a child's progression through childhood, adolescence, to adulthood. In more than one way, Alice's exploits are a timeless tale of a journey into the unconscious with its many perils, pleasant surprises, adventures, animal guides, and ideally, a corresponding increase in consciousness. During her journey, she tries to understand the ways of the world, authority relationships, the power games people play (how to make sense of seemingly arbitrary rules), the ambivalence of time, and the inevitability of death. At the same time, Wonderland represents a place of madness – a transitional space where the normal rules of behavior are no longer valid. As the Cheshire cat says, "We're all mad here." Life is full of riddles, or to quote William Blake, "this life's a fiction and is made up of contradiction."

In the last book in this series,[1] I observed the experiences of leaders on a rollercoaster ride through their professional and personal life. In this companion book, I follow them down the rabbit hole into the unknown, where, like Lewis Carroll's Alice, they find a dystopian Wonderland in which everyone seems to have gone mad and life functions according to its own crazy logic, throwing up all kinds of obstacles in the search for truth. Tumbling down the rabbit hole – in spite of all the nonsensical things that come about – is a metaphor for our efforts to become enlightened, to find the truth, to understand what is happening around us.

---

[1] Kets de Vries (2017).

Understanding what is happening around us has become more difficult than ever in the Age of Trump. What reassurance do we get from his declaration that his presidency is going to be "a beautiful thing"? Don't imperatives like "Build that wall" or "Lock her up" sound very much like "Off with her head"? Unfortunately, and unlike Alice, we are not going to wake up from a bad dream and discover that today's authority figures are "nothing but a pack of cards."

These essays are a personal effort at sense-making and spring from my current concern about the state of the world. The first part of this book looks at the psychodynamics of leadership in both a business and a political context. The ability of people in powerful positions to project and displace their personal neuroses into the public sphere has always been my major interest. The essays in Part I address contemporary issues. We're not exactly living in a universal "happy hour," and many of us are less than optimistic that we are creating a better world for our children. Have the people who decided to elect Trump as President forgotten the unspeakable darkness of World War 2, a conflict that was enabled by psychologically challenged leaders? As the philosopher George Santayana said, "Those who cannot remember the past are condemned to repeat it." In voting for a demagogue like Trump, people have demonstrated their ignorance of the consequence of putting their trust in perverse ideologies and autocratic leaders. Society's capacity to regress should never be underestimated. It is very easy to slip down the rabbit hole.

In Part II, I focus on the psychopathology of everyday life in organizations and look at the seemingly endless ways people can make a mess of things, including mega-pay packages, acting out, digital addiction, dysfunctional behavior, the darker side of human nature, and the quest for meaning.

But first, I take a brief look at two prominent themes in early twenty-first century life: the dystopian tendency and the darker side of leadership.

Dystopia

Dystopian fiction has been a recognized genre since the beginning of the twentieth century, and more recently dystopia has been the theme of an increasing number of films (*Blade Runner*, *The Matrix*), television series

(*The Man in the High Castle*), and computer games (*Call of Duty, Deus Ex*). These, and novels like George Orwell's *Nineteen Eighty-Four*, Aldous Huxley's *Brave New World*, and Margaret Atwood's *A Handmaid's Tale*, do not lift the spirits. These dystopian works depict dark visions of the future, highlighting the powerlessness of the individual in the face of coercive authorities. What's more, the lives of the people in these dystopian societies are characterized by endless drudgery with very little to hope for. One of the prevailing leitmotifs in these dystopian societies, preying on our somewhat paranoid psychological makeup (due to our evolutionary history), is that nobody can be trusted. Conspiracies are seen everywhere, turning these societies into living nightmares.

Ironically, the many advances in science and technology that we enjoy and take for granted today were achieved in the hope for a better future for humankind, yet what once seemed to be a prescription for progress has evolved into dystopian worries. In the pursuit of progress and knowledge, we often neglect to think through the moral, social, and environmental consequences of the actions we take.

The dystopian work that is so prevalent today can be seen as reflecting our prevailing concerns. Its paranoid, doom-ridden imagery is not being foisted on a resistant public. On the contrary, it illustrates the way cultural activity connects with current public sentiment. It is a response to the zeitgeist. What we should really be worrying about is the enthusiastic reception it receives.

The creators of these dystopian works paint Darwinian-like societies where belief in reason, human decency, equality, and sustainability is totally absent. They dramatize a realistic fear of how easily individuality could be stifled, personal freedom disappear, and political oppression enslave us. They show how ideological rigidity could imprison us, xenophobia turn to violence, and advanced technologies (such as robotization and artificial intelligence) turn on their creators. In the dystopian universe, genetic, financial, sociological, and digital engineering leads to apocalyptic consequences.

All these creative works draw on a number of our personal and social fears at an existential level: the loss of national identity, unemployment, lack of education, crime, and the (in)effectiveness of the democratic process. These fears are worsened by the awareness that we are now living in a one-percent society controlled by anonymous, fabulously wealthy, powerful oligarchies whose existence makes everyone else feel disenfranchised. Many worry that these elites have a dominant global influence, to the detriment of all others' well-being. It is a truism that great inequalities in wealth endanger open, democratic societies. No wonder that Donald Trump's campaign promise to "drain the swamp" became so popular.

Of course dystopias are nothing new; the imagery of dysfunctional societies has been with us for a very long time. Now, however, it seems much more pervasive.

The origins of many dystopian narratives can be traced back to the post-World War II era, when people worried about the possibility of nuclear annihilation, portrayed so well in the film *Dr. Strangelove or: How I Learned to Stop Worrying and Love the Bomb* (1964). Anxieties about the nuclear arms race also invoked worries about the probability of the catastrophic destruction of our natural environment. With proliferation of nuclear-capable countries, these worries persist. However, they are currently outweighed by the fear that general human activities could destroy the world, considering the way we are exhausting the Earth's resources and its ecosystem. Global warming is a growing concern. Psychologically speaking, the real danger of the consequences of global warming explains why some people so vehemently deny its existence. Unfortunately, denial is only a bromide. It doesn't change reality.

Add to these fears the dread of international terrorism, dictators that condone the killing of their own citizens, the aftershocks of financial meltdowns, rising levels of urban crime, the refugee crisis and immigrant issues, and threats of pandemic viruses and infections – all of which are trumpeted by round-the-clock news media – and it seems that what once seemed a fantasized dystopian future could easily become a terrible reality.

In our contemporary Cyber Age, the Internet – in spite of all its benefits – is increasingly being viewed with scepticism and suspicion. Many governments, helped by digital technology, seem to disregard basic human rights to privacy. The Edward Snowden saga, forcing the disclosure of numerous global surveillance programs, was a wake-up call about the exploitation of personal and official data. The safety and integrity of social media are coming under close scrutiny. We are increasingly fearful of being manipulated by forces that are beyond our awareness and control. Are the media subliminally brainwashing us, keeping us ignorant of what's really going on by feeding us factoids rather than facts? Have we been too complacent in using social media? Too trusting in putting so much personal information out there? Or too bamboozled by the delights of super-communication to think sensibly about the negative implications?

The Dark Side of Leadership

It's not hard to find examples of destructive leadership. We only have to look at what is happening in failed states such as South Sudan, the Democratic Republic of the Congo, Somaliland, Iraq, Afghanistan, Yemen, Syria, or Venezuela. And if what's happening there is not enough, in the United States we have the emergence of President Donald Trump, whose irresponsible behavior seems to know no bounds. Thanks to Trump's antics, the fear of nuclear warfare has once again become a leading international preoccupation. His quixotic and contradictory interactions with the North Korean dictator Kim Jong-un are as worrying, as they are puzzling. One minute he is dissing Kim as "little rocket man," the next he is cosying up to him in Singapore and apparently admiring Kim's style of leadership: "He speaks and his people sit up in attention. I want my people to do the same."[2] Equally disturbing is his confrontational stance toward Iran, going against the strategy of other Western nations. It's tempting to see his actions, like his appearance and oratory, as clownish, if not ridiculous. Most of his bizarre actions could be ignored if he were in charge of a minor country. But the United States is not a banana republic and Donald Trump is the most powerful individual in the world. His actions should be seen for what they are: extremely dangerous.

It's a truism to say that we get the leaders that we deserve. Looking at many of the leaders that rise to power, we could argue that the people who voted for them may have been uninformed, not realizing the consequences

---

[2] https://nbcnews.to/2ldZbEU

of their voting behavior. Often, when we select leaders, we like to see what they would like to see, rather than what is objectively most likely to happen. Although it is true to say that sometimes we need fantasy to survive reality, we should also realize that either we deal with the reality, or (like it or not) the reality will deal with us. Many people, however, prefer to hold on to delusionary fantasies rather than take a firm grip on what's likely to happen. Unfortunately, holding on to unrealistic fantasies about the future means being less prepared when the future arrives, and makes things more painful when they go wrong. While holding on to positive imagery may be comforting and relaxing in the short term, it will have devastating consequences in the long run.

An Outline

Keeping current global developments in mind, the first part of this book takes a macro-perspective in trying to better understand dystopian tendencies by focusing on leadership issues. And I start with Trump (or people like Trump), who in many ways can be taken as an archetype. His eligibility as a negative role model seems to be unmatchable, bringing as it does new unpleasant surprises every day. The reception of his activities underlines once more the human ability to rationalize contradictions and find sense in nonsense.

Drawing on Trump's example, the themes I discuss include the making of dictators, bullying, addiction to power, Trumpmania, the effects of malignant narcissism, the making of the ugly American, how to deal with narcissistic behavior, and how to successfully develop effective leaders.

The second part of the book looks beyond the vicissitudes of leadership to focus on the psychopathology of everyday life in organizations. Again, I discuss a variety of topics ranging from authentizotic organizations, to mega pay, family businesses, the role of the morosophe, the beggar's dilemma, shame, acting out, the importance of empathy, digital addiction, dealing with the dark side of human nature, partner choice, wisdom, and other matters relating to the endless ways people can mess up their lives.

Three Frameworks

We all know how faint the dividing line is between normality and neurosis – the perceived difference between normal and abnormal mental states is more apparent than real. We need to accept, however, that the gap between these two mental states is mostly imaginary and that the transition from one to the other is gradual and often almost imperceptible. Hints of pathology are evident in the everyday activities of everyone's life. The psychopathology that can be so clearly observed among the mentally ill is easily spotted (albeit to a lesser degree) in people who are perceived as normal. All of us are a bit crazy since all of us are haunted by deep inner conflicts that are not easily resolved. Inside all of us lurk wishes, desires, urges, and impulses that we are loath to acknowledge. A considerable part of our mental life will remain enigmatic to us, containing mysteries that can only be unraveled through psychological detective work. Things that appear to be coincidental or inexplicable might in fact be clues to some deeply hidden and tucked away truths. But in many instances, we may discover that there is not only a definite psychological cause for whatever seems surprising, but also that whatever is happening may have a logical, if initially not obvious, meaning. Surprisingly, much irrational human action turns out to have a rational explanation.

In that respect there is a great resemblance between the work of Sigmund Freud and Sherlock Holmes. As the great fictional detective put it, when trying to solve the mystery of the Hound of the Baskervilles, "The world is full of obvious things which nobody by any chance ever observes." He added that people see, but don't observe and hear but don't listen. In his various endeavors Sherlock Holmes makes it his business to know what other people don't, while realizing that nothing is as deceptive as an obvious fact. Don't always trust what you see. As we all know, even salt looks like sugar.

In trying to decipher the general emotional, intellectual, moral, and cultural patterns that influence our lives I have played Sherlock Holmes. Taking on this persona has helped me to analyze things beyond the obvious. It helped me understand that there are different levels of awareness. And although I try to look at every problem "without memory, desire, or understanding" (to use a well-known quote by the psychoanalyst Wilfred

Bion), I know that in my search for answers (conscious or unconscious) I'm very much guided by three frames of reference.

In the first place – given my training as a psychoanalyst – I am strongly influenced by a psychodynamic-systemic framework. I have a clinical orientation toward the vicissitudes of life. I have learned from experience that the exploration of below-the-surface phenomena – and how these dynamics influence our behavior, language, fantasies, and dreams – can be highly enlightening. The clinical paradigm is the framework through which I apply a psychodynamic lens to the study of the behavior of people in organizations. By making sense out of people's deeper wishes and fantasies – and showing how these fantasies influence behavior in the organizational world – I have found that this paradigm offers a very pragmatic way of discovering how executives and organizations really function.

As I have explored in much of my previous writing, the clinical paradigm consists of four basic premises. In the first place I argue that there is a *rationale behind every human act* – a logical explanation – even for actions that appear, at first glance, irrational. This point of view stipulates that all behavior has some kind of explanation. Because the explanation for what's happening may be elusive – inextricably interwoven with unconscious needs and desires – we need Sherlock Holmes's type of detective work to tease out hints and clues underlying perplexing behavior. Second, a great deal of mental life – feelings, fears, and motives – lies outside our conscious awareness but still affects conscious reality and even physical well-being. Like it or not, we all have blind spots. People aren't always aware of what they are doing, and much less *why* they are doing *what* they are doing. Though hidden from rational thought, the human unconscious affects (and in some cases even dictates) conscious reality. Even the most "rational" people have blind spots, and even the "best" people have a dark side – one they don't know, and may not *want* to know. The third premise states that nothing is more central to the way we are than the manner in which we regulate and express emotions. Emotions color experiences with positive and negative associations, creating preference in the choices we make and the way we deal with the world. Emotions also form the basis for the internalization of mental representations of the self and others that guide our relationships throughout life. However, the way we perceive and express emotions may change over time, as life experiences make their mark. The fourth premise underlying the clinical paradigm is that human development is an inter- and intrapersonal process. We are all products of our past experiences. These experiences, including the experiences provided by our early caregivers, continue to influence us throughout life. To better understand why we behave the way we do, it's helpful to recognize the degree to which we tend to re-enact childhood patterns in adulthood, even when such re-enactments are no longer appropriate.

The second frame of reference I have found valuable in my search to understand the changeability of human behavior is evolutionary psychology. This branch of psychology seeks to study behavior in the context of our evolutionary history. I have discovered that taking an evolutionary psychology perspective adds to the understanding of the complex patterns of causality in psychological and behavioral phenomena. Using this framework creates the awareness that the mind has been very much shaped by the pressures our prehistoric ancestors had to deal with to survive and reproduce. This conceptual framework adds to our appreciation of both the human body and the human mind, clarifying how evolutionary adaptations have affected behavior patterns, emotions, cognition, and brain structure. Mental and psychological traits – such as memory, perception, or language – can be viewed as the functional products of natural selection. With the help of these reconstructed problem-solving adaptations, we are also able to explain how these common behavioral roots are manifested in the various cultures around the world today. The application of evolutionary principles continues to permeate different sub-disciplines within psychology, including psychodynamic psychology, developmental psychology, cognitive theory, and neuroscience.

My third frame of reference is neuroscience. I have always looked for the most "scientific" explanations of why people do what they do. Neuroscience offers the very attractive possibility of joining the large number of people who hope to solve the deepest riddles of humanity through the study of the brain. Their wish is that, in opening a window into our mental life, neuroscience will help explain human nature. For many, brain-based explanations are superior to other ways of looking at human behavior.

Generally, neuroscience is associated with harder themes, such as physiology, neurons, hormones, receptors, and neurotransmitters, as opposed to the softer themes, such as thoughts, ideas, beliefs, emotions, and desires, that are found in more traditional psychology. I find intriguing the claims of many neuroscientists that specific patterns of neurological activity are correlated with certain behavior patterns. A very convincing argument in support of this is the brain-imaging process called functional magnetic resonance imaging (fMRI), which measures brain activity. But although what fMRI has to offer is very impressive, I sometimes wonder whether studying the fired-up areas of the brain explains what's going on inside a person with a great degree of accuracy. Will we find answers to the riddle of the mind merely by looking at a map of brain activity?

Even with the present state of scientific endeavor, it is still very difficult to capture the brain's exceedingly complex machinery through scans. Perhaps, there will always be certain patterns that are difficult to explain. So, even though I try to incorporate some neuroscientific findings into my detective work of human functioning, I believe we should be cautious about accepting many of the assertions made by neuroscientists. We should be aware of neurocentricity, that is, believing that human behavior can best be explained from the exclusive perspective of the brain structure. Mindless neuroscience is not going to be the answer to understand the functioning of the human mind. We might hope that neuroscience will not turn out to be an explanatory fad. That being said, in the years to come, neuroscience could evolve in such a way as to yield solid predictions about how genetics and brain conditions, and all of their complex aggregates and interactions, can influence a specific individual's specific choices at particular times.

The three frames of reference I outline here have been very useful to me in my role as Sherlock Holmes. They have helped me with the process of sense-making, contributing to a better understanding of the psychopathology of everyday life in organizations. Although I deal with extremely complex concepts, I set out to explore these ideas using easily understandable language. My experience of writing columns for newspapers has stood me in good stead here.

Final Comments

I have been an active reader throughout my life, and reading books has always been one of my major pleasures. Given this, it should come as no surprise that one of my major preoccupations (apart from teaching) has been writing books. Although I still write, I realize that there has been a shift in general reading behavior. Seeing my children and grandchildren immersed in social media, I wonder whether the Millennials and Generation Z still have the desire to read books. Is the digital revolution robbing these people of the act of reading books? Are these people forgoing the magic of reading? Are they investing most of their time in playing video games, social networking, texting, watching movies, and downloading apps for their smartphones and iPads? Do they think that reading books is for dullards? Do they get all the information they need through social media?

To a much lesser degree, the same pressures of dealing with the digital wave apply to me. Like everyone else, I feel like a victim of information overload. I am sometimes overwhelmed by an avalanche of information that has made it increasingly difficult to take time out and engage in the magic of reading novels. Slowly but surely my reading habits have been gravitating toward short, easily digestible material. This development has also affected my writing practice. Many of the chapters that make up this book were originally written as mini-articles (blogs) for the *Harvard Business Review* and *INSEAD Knowledge*. I found it a challenge to present complex ideas in a very condensed form. Given the way these pieces came about – and although I have aimed to create a logical sequence in the way they are presented here – each of these short chapters can be read as a standalone.

At the end of each chapter, I have added a short moral tale to illustrate the dilemma it presents. I hope these brief anecdotes will lead to some further self-questioning and help readers connect the text to their daily lives. Throughout our history, people have always tried to put important messages across through storytelling. Moral tales help us preserve our history and culture, passing it on to the next generation in a form that's easy to remember. Through these stories we communicate how to act toward one another, the things we value, and what is possible. We also use these stories to inculcate attitudes of tolerance; to stimulate courage, gratitude, and responsibility; to exercise emotional control, and to emphasize integrity.

Moral tales are also used to find solutions to difficult questions, such as why are we here? What is the purpose of our lives? What does it mean to be human? Some of these stories try to bring order and meaning to the chaos and randomness of life. They may help us to imagine possible futures. While we are immersed in these tales, we see the world through others' eyes. Moral tales are powerful tools, as they can be used to persuade people and change societies – with good and bad results.

I have also been affected by dystopian thoughts, but I recognize the importance of making the best of the present, and having hope for the future. If we dissect these dystopian works carefully, it's interesting to note that many protagonists in these tales have the courage to act for the good of humanity. Several of these stories are tales of how individuals surmount great challenges, deal with difficult situations, and take a stand against all that's wrong in society. Although they realize that life is full of struggle – and won't necessarily have a Disney ending – they also concede that there is always hope and that hope makes the present easier to bear. With hope we can take on the challenges we all have to deal with. Hope can bring light in the surrounding darkness; as the great novelist Dostoevsky put it, "To live without hope, is to cease to live." What these dystopian tales teach us is that when we join together, inspired by the hope for a better future, we will have a chance of survival. Only by working together can we set everything to rights.

We should remind ourselves that big things tend to have small beginnings. If we take life one day at a time, we can handle just about anything. If each of us takes a small step every day toward making things better, we may eventually get where we want to be. We could also remind ourselves that the nice thing about fictionalized dystopian worlds is that we can experience vicariously what might happen, while leaving open the opportunity to do something to avert it. I hope this collection of essays will be read with this kind of spirit in mind.

2

Do You Want to Be Led by a Dictator?

Every dictator is an enemy of freedom, an opponent of law.
—Demosthenes
*It was one of the greatest errors in evaluating dictatorship to say that the
dictator forces himself on society against its own will. In reality, every dictator
in history was nothing but the accentuation of already existing state ideas
which he had only to exaggerate in order to gain power.*
—Wilhelm Reich

There was much jubilation after Peter was elected president. People were overjoyed to finally have a new face, rather than a member of the old guard, leading the country. The new president had presented a vision for the future that gave them hope. But as time passed, things didn't turn out as expected. The combination of position and disposition (that is, Peter's personality) turned out to be a very toxic brew. The power that came with the position of president seemed to have gone to Peter's head, having a strange effect on him. Not that the new president changed his behavior immediately. It was a process that happened very subtly.

The first sign that raised concern was when Peter began putting people close and loyal to him into key positions, in spite of their questionable

© The Author(s) 2019
M. F. R. Kets de Vries, *Down the Rabbit Hole of Leadership*,
https://doi.org/10.1007/978-3-319-92462-5_2

abilities. Many of the people who had voted for him wondered at this blatant nepotism, but continued to give him the benefit of the doubt. Unfortunately, that wasn't all. What caused even greater concerns was his adversarial attitude toward any form of criticism, especially through the mainstream press. The new president clearly did not welcome critical coverage. As he began to arrest journalists, many media outlets began to practice self-censorship. Peter's speeches, in which he alluded to conspiracies and made insinuations about enemies of the state, did nothing to help the political climate. To add to the dark cloud over his presidency, he harped on about threats to the people's way of life: too many criminals and foreigners were impinging on the values and livelihood of law-abiding citizens. But, he assured all and sundry, they were in safe hands. He would be their great protector. He would do everything in his power to keep the country safe; he would be tough and stay the course. Some astute political observers pointed out that this was a tried and tested tactic to get a sizable portion of the public on his side. They also noted that, step-by-step, their new president was taking away the fundamental liberties of the country and its people.

Dictators – whether they led tribes, fiefdoms, countries, cults, religions, or organizations – have been with us from our early Palaeolithic roots onward. We have always been attracted to people who appear strong; many view dictators as beacons of stability in a very turbulent world. Some are even prepared to give up their freedoms for an imagined sense of stability and protection. The powerful attraction of dictators is increased by their ability to create the illusion that they will restore whatever greatness is wished for.

The title *dictator* dates back to Roman times when in situations of emergency the Senate could suspend normal political processes, forego elections, and appoint one person (the dictator) to be in charge of everything. The dictator was entitled to rule by decree. Generally speaking, social unrest has always been the feeding ground for dictators. Periods of economic depression, political, or social chaos would often lead to the belief that liberal and open democracies were fallible political systems. Consequently, times of social unrest would give dictators the opportunity to take on the role of savior and when conditions would allow it, take power by *coup d'état* or other means. But while posturing as high-minded, inspired candidates for change, dictators would also present unrealistic ideas and plans, and make promises to solve even the most hopeless of situations. Given their rhetorical skills, their populist demagoguery would seduce sizable numbers of the population. However, if we look beyond the superficial spectacle and critically assess what these dictators were actually doing, we quickly realize that most of their inflated promises are just hot air.

Dictators leverage a number of social processes and dynamics to gain influence and followership. First, they are extremely talented at inflaming the wish to believe. Their cries of patriotism and righteousness mirror the message that the populace wants to hear. And people's unquestioning acceptance of a dictator's rhetoric is rooted in humankind's most pervasive bias – the confirmation bias. Under this bias, we interpret evidence in ways that are consistent with our ideas and desires, while discounting contradictory evidence. The confirmation bias simplifies complexity when processing information, but it also can be seen as a form of neurological laziness. As expert manipulators, dictators take advantage of this cognitive shortcut. As Adolf Hitler used to say, "How fortunate for governments that the people they administer don't think." Donald Trump made an equally troublesome observation: "I love the poorly educated."

Identification with the Aggressor

While practicing their Machiavellian games, dictators are especially good at targeting groups of socially and economically vulnerable people who tend to be poorly educated, have little access to information, and feel confused, insecure, and disempowered. They exploit the rage and frustration of those that who feel left behind. Under these circumstances they seduce mentally vulnerable people. Through the psychological process of identification with the aggressor (explored further in Chap. 5), they see in this strong man or woman both a reflection of themselves, and also the promise of some kind of victory that will redeem them from their downtrodden state. Given dictators' talent for illusions and magical thinking – packaging the right messages – their constituency is easily brainwashed.

Whatever the societal wrongs, dictators are very adept at stirring up the impulse to blame and scapegoat. They play off the primitive defense mechanism of splitting, by positioning issues in terms of in- and out-groups, magnifying external threats, and fanning collective paranoia. At the same time, they offer themselves as steadfast saviors. Their followers buy into their simplistic, binary propositions, and align themselves with the good fight against evil. Subsequently, people under the sway of dictators become intolerant toward those they perceive as different.

Over and above this, to ensure the righteousness of their cause, dictators go to great lengths to silence dissidents and doubters. Dictatorial regimes have eyes and ears everywhere and people either fall in line or face the music. To ensure compliance, dictatorial systems use fear (executed by enforcers) as a primary tool. People are constantly reminded of their enemies, of the threats around them, and of the consequences of straying from the party line. Over time, fear can become so embedded in the fabric of everyday life that people may not even notice it.

Dictators quickly learn the value of indoctrination through propaganda and mind control. They realize that controlling information is essential to maintaining their hold on power, so they try to centralize all mainstream media. They make sure that everything positive is attributed to them, while all negative news is ascribed to enemies of the state. With such an incessant propaganda machine, it's no wonder dictators become an integral part of everyone's life; it becomes unimaginable that anything is possible without their presence. When it comes to elections, dictators resort to a whole bag of tricks – curtailing press freedom, limiting the opposition's ability to campaign, spreading misinformation, and manipulating the final outcome. Dictators also ensure that no social frameworks and institutions promote and sustain liberty and serve as countervailing forces. If these institutions exist, they do everything in their power to destroy them.

The Origins of Dictators

Dictators don't come out of nowhere. Their spawning grounds are social and economical disorder. They know that in stressful situations, people resort to a state of dependency, and will regress to looking for simplistic solutions to their problems, bond with powerful leaders, and give them unquestioning loyalty and obedience in exchange for direction and protection.

But while it is easy to vilify dictators, we should also ask the more difficult question of who is responsible for their existence? In more than one way, we (the people) enable them. We (the people) are the enemy. After all, a dictator cannot function without followers. And although we may not admit it aloud, it's attractive to have others tell us what to do, what's right, what's wrong, and that there's nothing to worry about. But we seem to forget that the abdication of personal responsibility comes with the loss of our freedom of expression, the derailment of democratic processes, and the loss of our personal integrity. In complying with a dictator's wishes, we may receive favors, usually material, in return. And so we are gradually corrupted, benefiting from the dictator's favors, and reinforcing and perpetuating the autocratic system that he or she has put into place.

From the supply side, there is never going to be a lack of wannabe dictators. There will always be people who are attracted to power and most of them have a specific personality makeup that predisposes them to dictatorship. Many past and contemporary dictators suffer from extraordinarily high levels of narcissism, psychopathy, and paranoia. They have an inflated sense of self-importance, see themselves as special, and feel entitled to the admiration of others. In many instances, their narcissistic disposition tends to be malignant (I describe this further in Chap. 4). Because they often have difficulty empathizing with the needs of others, and are not beholden to feelings of guilt or remorse, dictators are capable of committing unspeakable atrocities, brutalities, and crimes.

Eventually, however, dictatorial individuals become isolated, living in an echo chamber that amplifies what they want to hear. Because of their charismatic appeal, they attract sycophants who help nurture their megalomania. However, this creates a closed circle, in which dictators can become self-delusional and lose touch with reality.

Creating a Responsible Electorate

We might have thought that we have seen the demise of dictatorships today, but how wrong could we be? We are currently witnessing the gathering of a perfect storm. Even in many established democracies, the slide down the slippery slope to dictatorship is becoming a real threat. Accelerated globalization has created anxieties and fears among large groups of people who feel disenfranchised, particularly in the West, where many have become worried about a non-Western, Islamic "invasion." As a result, identity politics has re-emerged with all its xenophobic overtones. The increase in immigration has given rise to people's fears; many have become fearful of losing their sense of identity. The threat (and the reality) of terrorism have aggravated the situation. Each day, thanks to powerful mass communication, brings fresh news of yet another atrocity. At the same time people are trying to cope with a digital wave that has increased the fear of professional obsolescence, a concern that contributes to a great deal of additional anxiety. It is not surprising that when people believe that the current system is incapable of solving the prevalent social problems in society, they will be more inclined to give up power to some kind of savior that they imagine can solve all that's wrong in society. Given all this, the overriding question becomes: can we prevent dictators from achieving power?

As a kind of preventive maintenance, we need to recognize potential dictators before they stealthily compromise and destroy our lives. Once they are in power, it's too late. Turning the tide at that point is mission impossible.

Given that the populace enables the dictator, the populace can equally pre-empt the dictator rising to power. But the prerequisite is having a democracy built on a mature and well-informed public that's prepared to respect different opinions and recognizes the importance of a well-functioning society. This means having a proactive and critical populace that knows how to distinguish between real and fake news – that has access to reliable sources of information, and is able to listen to different points of view and manage ambiguities. This necessitates that a country's potential electorate is informed by a variety of news sources, not a few, restricted ones. As things are now, many people find it difficult to distinguish between real and fake news, especially when the American Propagandist in Chief is so fond of declaring which is which. To distinguish reality from fantasy it is essential that the populace is informed about what electoral candidates represent. This implies a voting population that's mobilized and will engage, rather than deciding that voting is somebody else's business. In short, preventing dictators from coming to power requires a population that cares about its liberty – people who have a vision of what an open society looks like.

Preventing the rise of autocrats necessitates having powerful and independent institutions with properly segregated branches of authority and oversight that follow the rule of law. The government, the head of state, the legislature, the courts, the press, and the electorate should be independent of one another.

Of course, there's always the question whether dictators in the making can be "cured?" I'm afraid to say it's not likely. Historical experience has proven otherwise. Also, from a clinical perspective, most psychotherapists, psychoanalysts, and psychiatrists believe that dictators (in particular the psychopathic ones) are untreatable. Countervailing powers (in the form of robust institutional structures and a conscious electorate) can only hope to provide preventive intervention, not effective treatment.

In his most famous film *The Great Dictator*, Charlie Chaplin satirizes Nazism and Adolf Hitler while playing the role of a misbegotten barber turned absolute ruler of the fictional country of Tomainia. Chaplin's efforts to warn people about the dangers of dictatorship were very opportune, given that the film was made in 1940, when the world was exposed to another perfect storm. At the end of the film, Chaplin delivers an impassioned speech asking the populace to unite and fight dictatorships. He says:

> You, the people, have the power to make this life free and beautiful, to make this life a wonderful adventure... In the name of democracy let us use that power; let us all unite. Let us fight for a new world – a decent world that will give men a chance to work – that will give youth a future and old age a security...
>
> Dictators free themselves but they enslave the people! Now let us fight to fulfil that promise! Let us fight to free the world – to do away with national barriers – to do away with greed, with hate and intolerance. Let us fight for a world of reason, a world where science and progress will lead to all men's happiness.

Unfortunately, we are still far from the kind of world that Chaplin had in mind. When we look at our present world leaders, many of them are making huge efforts to endanger the democratic processes. Narrow-minded nationalism, xenophobia, greed, destructive power plays, and unimaginable violence are present everywhere. It makes it even timelier to strive for the kind of world envisioned by Chaplin in *The Great Dictator*.

Here's a story of my own. It concerns a dictator who had recently made a new conquest. Following his victory, and feeling extremely pleased with himself for having enlarged his territory, he visited a wise man and asked his advice. "Given all my conquests, I would like a new title to celebrate my achievements. I think my new title should include the word 'Heaven.' There have been many conquerors with titles like From Heaven, Heaven's Warrior, or Sent from Heaven."

The response of the wise man was, "How about 'Heaven Forbid'?"

3

Trumpmania

My IQ is one of the highest—and you all know it! Please don't feel so stupid
or insecure; it's not your fault.
—Donald Trump
I think I am actually humble. I think I'm much more humble than you
would understand.
—Donald Trump

Frank Capra's Academy Award winning film, *Mr. Smith Goes to Washington*,
is about a one-man campaign against dishonest politics. James Stewart,
the leading character, plays an average Joe and a naïve, self-conscious ide-
alist stalwartly fighting the corrupt politics in the US Senate. But in spite
of the bullying and bribing by crooked politicians, he sticks to his values
and social convictions and triumphs in the end. Mr. Smith is making a
humane difference.

Then we have Donald Trump. Given his attraction to one-man rule,
Trump is the epitome of autocratic behavior and self-pandering, not
social justice. He is also a larger-than-life lesson in personality theory, an
unholy alliance of a narcissistic personality disorder blended with psychopathic behavior. Presently, he is running the world's largest reality show.

© The Author(s) 2019
M. F. R. Kets de Vries, *Down the Rabbit Hole of Leadership*,
https://doi.org/10.1007/978-3-319-92462-5_3

Typically, people suffering from a narcissistic personality disorder have a grandiose sense of self-importance. Their world centers on power, success, and appearances. They exaggerate their achievements and talents and are cocky, self-centered, and manipulative. In addition, they feel a strong sense of entitlement, always expecting special treatment. Furthermore, many narcissists lack empathy. And behind this mask of super-confidence, we often find a person with a fragile self-esteem, vulnerable to the slightest criticism.

In terms of psychopathy, many of these people may appear normal, even charming, but also display persistent antisocial behavior. Their lack of conscience and empathy, and their inability to feel attached to people, contributes to a predatory lifestyle. They manipulate others by playing to their emotions. They feel little or no regret or remorse for people caught in their venomous web. (These two behavior patterns are treated in more detail in Chap. 4.)

Trump fits this unholy dyad to a T. The king of mixed signals is famous for his capacity for self-aggrandizement, gets off-balance and becomes highly defensive when he perceives slights, and attacks and denigrates everyone who disagrees with him. Spite, envy, and vindictiveness are part of the package. He has no empathy for others, is careless with facts, and has a Teflon capacity when confronted with information he finds disagreeable. He also thrives on conflict. Fighting with people – wanting to win whatever it is – makes him feel truly alive. As I have said previously, this kind of acting out would raise fewer flags if he were running for office in a banana republic. We are talking, however, about the highest office in the most important country in the world. His presidency has implications not only for the United States, but also for the rest of the planet. Is he the kind of person we want to have with a finger on the nuclear button?

Donald Trump is who he is. But the greater conundrum is why he has the zealous support of so many people. Trump, a wounded and quite disturbed individual, has become attractive to millions of Americans. What are the underlying psychological and group dynamics at play? Taking a more in-depth look, we can identify processes such as regression, dependency, idealization, the wish to believe, splitting, and identification with the aggressor.

From an evolutionary psychological perspective, our tendency to deify people in leadership positions is deeply embedded in the human psyche.

The contributing factor could be our evolutionary history – eons of developmental programming that took place to ensure survival during the early days of *Homo sapiens*. When we think of our Palaeolithic ancestors, we should remind ourselves of the many dangers they lived with. No wonder, given their vulnerability, that saviors were in great demand. This evolutionary thread might explain why we have a primitive tendency to regress, to submit ourselves to the dominance of the leader of the pack.

Taking a more developmental point of view, our disposition to regress into states of dependency can also be accentuated by our experiences in infancy. When we are small and relatively helpless, we believe in our parents' omniscience. In the process of becoming a person, we continue to idealize and identify with competent, admired others. Eventually, as part of the process of growing up, we come to realize the importance of relying on one's own resources. In crisis situations, however, and in periods of high stress, we tend to regress to the old pattern of dependency and to look for strong people to guide and at times deliver us.

Given where we come from, this longing for saviors is part and parcel of our psychological makeup. And when social and cultural institutions are disintegrating, the attraction of powerful leaders becomes ever more tempting. Caught up in an emotional whirlwind of uncertainty, anxiety and fear, we become less selective in both thought and action; in short, we become very gullible. We may slip into child-like ways of perceiving, feeling, and thinking, even to the point of abdicating personal responsibility. Under these conditions, manipulative leaders (adept at simplification and dramatization) rise up by riding on these vulnerabilities to present themselves as merchants of hope.

Furthermore, Trump knows how to use his charisma, charm, and notoriety to enhance idealization processes. Idealization is a defense mechanism whereby we overestimate someone's desirable qualities and underestimate their limitations. Once again, this defense mechanism starts in childhood when children try to cope with feelings of weakness, inadequacy, and isolation by developing the interpersonal strategy of idealization, compensating for feelings of powerlessness. But when we engage in such hero worship – when we maximize virtues, and minimize flaws – we hold on to the unrealistic belief that there is a person out there with the power to make things better. These regressive psychological processes partially explain why the Trumpmaniacs, in spite of all his outrageous peccadillos, keep cheering him on.

Trump also encourages wishful thinking – holding on to hopeful beliefs that have no concrete foundation. When we are caught in this wish to believe pattern, we are more likely to find evidence that supports our position, and filter out any evidence to the contrary. Again, this is the confirmation bias – looking for information that confirms pre-existing beliefs. By making illusory promises, people like Trump turn into con-men, spinning their empty promises into seductive tales.

Another quality of Trump is his talent for splitting. Splitting (some-times called all-or-nothing thinking) implies the polarization of beliefs, events, actions, and people, in other words, seeing the world as either black or white. It means cherishing absolutes and failing to bring together the positive and negative qualities of an individual, situation or issue into a cohesive, realistic whole. Splitting is very attractive because it offers uncomplicated, simplistic solutions to highly complex human situations. This divide and conquer strategy is one of the more effective tactics that people like Trump have in their arsenal to manipulate and control the people who identify with them.

The Theater of Obsequiousness

Idealizing a person like Trump is one thing, but this process can go one step further through the psychological process of identification with the aggressor (see Chap. 5). Although Trump's extreme personality and ideas might frighten many of us, some people are drawn to the protection he seems to offer. Instead of perceiving him as an enemy or threat, they con-quer their fear by trying to become like him and adopting rather than resisting or challenging his position. Trump has been compared to a Mafia boss, an observation made by the former FBI Director, James Comey.[1] He describes "[t]he silent circle of assent" that surrounds the President. "The boss in complete control. Loyalty oaths. The us-versus-them world view. The lying about all things, large and small, in service to some code of loyalty." If that's what the rigor amounts to at the court of

---

[1] Comey (2018).

Trump, obsequiousness might be the wisest survival strategy. However, the Mafia boss analogy may not be completely appropriate. The present White House seems to be more like a medieval court, with its cliques and coerced displays of fealty, all taking place under the somewhat paranoid eye of Trump and his closest family members. Given what they are up against, his courtiers have figured out that the only way to survive Trump's peculiar reign is through flattery taken to the extreme.

The people of Trump's inner circle have been surpassing each other in expressing their subservience at an unmatched, and highly creative level. For example, the outgoing House Speaker, Paul Ryan, praised Trump's "exquisite leadership." Senator Orrin Hatch declared that "one of the great privileges of my life [is] to stand here on the White House lawn with the President of the United States who I love and appreciate so much." And Stephen Miller (a major Trump aide), "sees a man who [is] a political genius." Nobody, however, has attained the glorious heights of obsequiousness of Vice-President Mike Pence, who has thanked Trump "for fulfilling miracles," and credited him with "restoring American credibility on the world stage, spurring record-setting optimism." And as a final touch, Pence was kind enough to add that "serving the President is the greatest privilege of my life."

It goes without saying that a culture of obsequiousness doesn't attract the best and the brightest – quite the opposite. Even more troublesome is that people who engage in flattery are often those with even darker personality traits – the opportunists, the lazy, the power-hungry, the greedy, even the psychopathic and sociopathic. The latter may view the people who crave flattery as a potential source of money, power, and influence. Such connivers take advantage of the fact that flattery has the power to influence, corrupt, undermine, and deceive. Those they flatter are seen as easy pickings – theirs for the taking. In their hands, flattery can turn into a lethal weapon against the undiscerning.

There are many risks when leaders fall under the spell of flattery. Driven by their narcissistic needs, they may not pick up on the agenda hidden in the obsequious behavior of subordinates. They may not understand their ulterior motives. Adding to this disturbing equation is that (consciously or unconsciously) flattery tends to stick. Sustained flattery can move into the unconscious with devastating results. No wonder that it contributes to ineffective reality-testing and creates a world of make-believe, in which important decisions become sub-optimal.

Furthermore, when people suck up to Trump and other autocratic leaders (while trying to appear genuine), they lose parts of themselves. Flattery comes at the cost of authenticity. Actions (even when there is a modicum of sympathy for the person they are working for) are too much driven by personal gain. Of course, we could argue that to have a chance for success in organizational life, we have no choice but to resort to some obsequiousness, to get people in powerful positions to like and value us. What is surprising, however, is how many members of Team Trump go to such lengths to compromise their reputations and their dignity. Given his many improprieties, a willingness to serve Trump has turned into a serious test of character – with a high moral price for those who pass the test.

When leaders make obsequious behavior the norm, thoughtful actions are thrown out of the window. Groupthink prevails – a phenomenon whereby the members of the in-group are so eager to agree with each other that decisions go unchallenged and are ultimately of poor quality. When groupthink comes to the fore, pleasing the power-holder becomes more important than making the best decisions. People who aspire to speaking truth to power are strongly discouraged; any form of disagreement becomes unacceptable and carries the risk of retribution. For survival purposes, those that report to "great men" refrain from expressing doubt, judgment, or disagreement with the consensus. They accept unquestioningly the gospel truth spread by the leader and his inner circle. Even more dangerous is that the leader and his inner entourage may not question ethically dubious decisions and actions. The ethical consequences of group decisions are ignored as long as they further their cause.

Furthermore, narcissistic leaders too often create a Darwinian soup-like environment where everyone is out for themselves. The survival of the fittest mentality is a breeding ground for paranoia and anxiety. The culture of fear makes people resort to social defenses to deal with stress in the workplace – they turn a blind eye to difficult emotions, topics or relations. By wanting not to see, they create the illusion of certainty and safety. In reality, they are participating in an unconscious collusion to protect themselves against the tension prevalent at work. Unfortunately, this protection comes at the expense of carrying out their real tasks. It also prevents them from taking the kinds of constructive action that would eliminate the sources of stress or threat in the first place.

As we can all see, the Trumps of this world have been very successful in using and manipulating these complex psychological dynamics. They have a masterful ability to spread false or exaggerated beliefs to create collective delusions and dependencies. They know how to use the mass media, rumors, cultural beliefs, and stereotypes to their advantage. Adept at exploiting the power of suggestion, they know how to redefine events and circumstances in their own distorted ways. Creating the illusion of their charismatic infallibility, they attract people like moths to a flame. Unfortunately, followers who relinquish autonomous thinking and buy into the collective delusions of such manipulative leaders rarely recognize the destructive path they are on. They want so desperately to believe the proffered images of unlimited power, regal grandeur, and awe-inspiring majesty that they fail to see what the leader really stands for and what the broader consequences are. They cheerfully shake their hand and cement a Faustian bargain, not recognizing the high price that eventually has to be paid. For example, the presidential reality show in the United States has turned into a strange and very worrisome theater of the absurd for non-Americans and many US citizens alike. While the US has always played an important role in maintaining the global world order, we are presently faced with very regressive and troubling behavior.

Collective Angst

The allure of a person like Trump may be a reflection of the underlying angst and anger of what has been happening to the American dream, a fantasy that has formed an important part of the inner landscape of Americans for many decades. This dreamscape views the United States as a land of unlimited opportunities – a place where almost anyone can be successful if he or she is prepared to work hard. It represents the rags to riches story – where a paperboy can become a millionaire. Furthermore, an important part of the American dream is people's belief that their children will have a better life than they have had. This dream represents not only a quest for security, wealth, or material abundance, but also stronghold principles of self-actualization and personal fulfillment.

But something has gone horribly wrong with the American dream. For many Americans, life has become harder, not easier. The belief that each generation will be better off compared to the previous one is rapidly disappearing.[2] When we study demographic trends, we can see that the middle class in the United States is in steady decline. The cost of living is going up while for a large segment of the US population, income, net worth, and the quality of jobs is going down. To many, a living wage and security in retirement has turned into a pipe dream. Years of downsizing, lay-offs, the flight of manufacturing jobs overseas, and the proliferation of low-paid service jobs have changed the job market and conditions of life. The harsh new reality is that many Americans find it hard to pay their bills and the probability that their children will get ahead in life is no longer a given. Today, a college education requires serious financial resources, and many students end up with a mountain of debt. Meanwhile, surveys of one-percenters (the top 1% of the population by wealth) show that the rich have become richer.[3] Top CEOs make at least 300 times more than the median employee (see Chap. 11). The wealthiest 10% of US households now control nearly 75% of all wealth in the country.[4] Far from empowering the lives of ordinary people, technology and globalization only seem to have undermined the lives of many American people, eliminating traditional blue-collar and middle-class sources of employment. Social mobility has stalled.

These social developments have affected the mental state of large segments of the US population and brought about feelings of unfairness and disenfranchisement. Many US citizens are angry with the politicians in Washington spanning social institutions such as the government, churches, the legal system, and the business world.[5] The trust that many had in their political representatives has evaporated. The extremely regressive political positions taken by Trump and his coterie are a reflection of their anxieties about their current and future state.

---

[2] Pew Research Center (2015).
[3] Pew Research Center (2015).
[4] Global Research (2015).
[5] The Esquire (2016).

We should not dismiss these concerns. Unfortunately, there is much truth in what many Americans are saying: that their political system is rigged and that many politicians are beholden not to the people but to Wall Street and large donors. It can be argued that the existence of super-PACs suggests that something has gone horribly wrong with the American political system – that the American dream is exactly that: only a dream. No wonder that so many voters are looking for people free from the special interests of corporate America. No wonder that we are seeing the rise of populist candidates, inappropriate as their messages might be. Their provocative and extreme platforms signify the electorate's sense of powerlessness to influence the things that matter in their lives. It explains why anti-establishment political demagogues, and true con-artists like Trump, who offer nothing substantial in the way of solutions to very complex world problems, have come to power.

The Art of the Con

One of the more remarkable characters in Gaetano Donizetti's popular opera *L'Elisir d'Amore* is the traveling confidence artist, Dr. Dulcamara, a connoisseur of the foibles of human nature, who sells his fraudulent bottled cure-alls to believers. Everybody is drawn to his hypnotic sales pitch, to great comical effects. Unfortunately, this behavior is not limited to comic opera. Trump and Dulcamara are interchangeable. They both thrive on the anxiety of the populace.

In their (conscious or unconscious) attempts at demagoguery, Dulcamara-types like Trump are encouraging Americans to interpret evidence in ways that are consistent with their various desires. As effective snake oil salesmen, they want people to believe what they want to believe. They insidiously encourage segments of the American population to listen to arguments that support their position – helped by selected media outlets – while discounting evidence that they don't like to hear. No wonder that bigotry, protectionism, and nostalgia for a past that may never have truly existed, are raising their ugly heads.

The Danger Signs

So how easy is it to recognize con men? Unfortunately, they come in all shapes and sizes and look pretty much like everyone else. But that being said, there are a few warning signs that can alert us when we encounter these psychopathic personalities. For a start, we should be on guard when someone has inflated credentials. Con men not only paint an exaggerated picture of their accomplishments, they are also masters (when it is in their interest) in making us feel special. Beware of the charisma, charm, and magnetism that they can project. Beware, too, if their stories seem too good to be true. Always listen to the sceptic voice in your head. Also, con men thrive on conflict – they like to create a sense of emergency – so don't fall back on quick decisions. When pushed, it's wiser to take your time. Repeat the words of Groucho Marx: "The secret of life is honesty and fair dealing. If you can fake that, you've got it made." Con artists get away with what they get away with because the people they dupe are ashamed of their own blindness and naivety.

Let me end with an anecdote about Trump. The morning after Trump issues another of his anti-Obama regulations, three local Democrats are expressing their dislike for his administration.

One of them says, "He's a fool." The other adds, "He is a womanizer. He grabs women left and right." The third rejoins, "And he's a thief. He takes people's money."

At that moment, a police officer appears out of nowhere and says, "Right! I heard what you Democrats said about Trump, and I'm taking you straight to jail. How dare you insult the President."

"Trump?" says one of the Democrats. "But we're talking about Vladimir Putin." "Oh," the police officer says. "Well, next time, choose your words more carefully. I mean, I heard you say fool, womanizer, and thief – so I naturally assumed you were talking about Trump."

It has often been said that people get the leaders they deserve. We can only hope that sanity will eventually prevail in the United States.

4

The Ugly American

America is great because she is good. If America ceases to be good, America will cease to be great.
—Alexis de Tocqueville
One of the key problems today is that politics is such a disgrace. Good people don't go into government.
—Donald Trump

It is easy, sometimes almost automatic, to put groups of people into categories. It simplifies our lives. Take Europe, and its myriad stereotypes, as an example. In a tongue-in-cheek way, hell has been described as a place where the Germans are the policemen, the British are the cooks, the French are the mechanics, the Swiss are the lovers, the Swedes are the comedians, the Dutch are the fashion designers, the Greeks run the government, and the Italians organize everything. This whimsical illustration shows that stereotyping is a relatively quick if reductionist way to understand the behavior of others. As a cognitive and emotive short cut, it reduces the amount of mental processing we have to do by relying on simplistic generalizations.

© The Author(s) 2019
M. F. R. Kets de Vries, *Down the Rabbit Hole of Leadership*,
https://doi.org/10.1007/978-3-319-92462-5_4

Incomplete as these kinds of categorizations may be, stereotypes tend to stick. They caricaturize ideas about collective personality and have an enduring quality. However, real danger lies when we start treating people on the basis of these stereotypes.

Opinion shapers like political leaders tend to rely on and reinforce stereotypes in their discourse. Given the positions they occupy, their behavior can become larger than life. We frequently take the actions of a country's leaders as representative of the character and beliefs of its people. For example, the behavior and actions of former Italian prime minister Silvio Berlusconi underscores our stereotyping of Italians as lecherous, over-sexed (a nod to Berlusconi's bunga bunga parties), endemically corrupt, and being in bed with the Mafia. It's fair to say that 20 years with Berlusconi at the center of Italy's political system did have a very negative impact on the country's brand image. A single leader became the personification of the "*brutto italiano*." He certainly underscored the existing stereotype.

Italy may be an important country on the world stage, but it is nowhere in comparison to America, the most powerful (economically and militarily) country in the world. In that role, America has always been a very attractive target for stereotyping. We are always ready to debate what the American "brand" is all about.

Branding became a preoccupation in 1958, when William J. Lederer and Eugene Burdick published their novel, *The Ugly American*, a collection of interwoven stories about the US diplomatic corps, set in the thinly disguised country of Sarkhan (easily recognizable as Vietnam). The novel highlights how ineffectively US officials dealt with Sarkhan's culture and operating conditions. Their behavior reflected the narrowly US-centric, ignorant, loud, tone-deaf, and disrespectful American abroad.

The novel was a national bestseller and had a significant impact through its devastating indictment of US foreign policy. It had a greater influence on policy-setting in the US than any other work of political fiction. To underline this point, when *The Ugly American* was published, it was praised by John F. Kennedy (then a senator), along with several other prominent figures. Kennedy liked it so much that he took out a full-page advertisement in *The New York Times*, saying the novel was a compelling critique of "the Americans who go overseas for the various governmental agencies, their activities abroad, and the policies they are entrusted to carry out." Subsequently, he sent a copy of the novel to every member of the Senate, as a cautionary tale against negative stereotypes, hoping that it would influence their policy-making practices.

Sixty years later, President Donald Trump is a star performer in *The Ugly American* reality show. It's one thing to have a leader who takes part in bunga bunga parties, but quite another to have a psychologically challenged individual with a finger on the nuclear button. The way Trump is conducting foreign policy augurs *The Ugly American* all over again. And if that were not enough, the Trump era suggests the prescience of another influential political novel, George Orwell's *Nineteen Eighty-Four*. A major reason for the novel's current resurgence on the bestseller list is Trump, who has sold America as a dystopian society, where threats from external enemies are ever present, simplistic binary slogans replace reflective debate, lies become alternative facts (or factoids), and where mind and reality control replace evidence and historical truth.

On the trail from George Washington up to Barack Obama, no US political leader has acted with such incompetence, impulsiveness, and contempt for the responsibility of leadership. No wonder that a host of political analysts have described Trump as "uniquely unqualified" to be the President of the United States due to his lack of political experience, lack of knowledge about public policy, attention deficit, and unwillingness to learn or listen to good advice. Trump is vain, a bully, an unrepentant liar, and indulges in outbursts of rage and feelings of vengeance. No other American President in modern history has demonstrated this degree of character pathology. His buffoon-like behavior has led to some referring to him as the "Clown-in-Chief" running a Grand Guignol regime.

The whole world is watching in disbelief as Trump heads up a new kind of very dangerous reality show. Despite Trump's racism, misogyny, and disrespectful behavior, Republican leaders (and many foreign dignitaries, for that matter) are too opportunistic to take a stand against him. They have learned that, with Trump, obsequiousness wins the day. Taking a one-down position and laying on flattery is critical for survival.

We have always been inclined to cheer on the unexpected outsider who promised to beat the system. There are many Americans who admire Trump and his stated mission to "drain the swamp" of US politics. But it takes a particular sort of gall to declare a loss of almost a billion dollars in his own businesses while promising to be the savior of the economy. It takes even more gall to brag about being "smart" enough to avoid paying basic income tax for decades. Yet Trump keeps getting away with it. People continue to buy into this ugly American's tale.

Deep down inside, many people know that they are being suckered. But in spite of the overwhelming evidence that Trump is pulling a fast one, they still find it hard to acknowledge that it is happening. Unfortunately, many people become willing victims of this sort of scam. The power of con artists is that they don't force us to do anything. On the contrary, victims buy into the con game of their own free will. Some may even volunteer and propagate the cause. And after the damage is done, it is not easy to admit having been a victim of a scam (a nod to the Republican leadership here).

As I wrote in Chap. 2, con men like Trump thrive in times of crisis, transition, and change when people pin their hopes on the leader who looks most like a savior and adopt a dependency stance. To maintain power, con men inflame and magnify the crisis. The more vivid the dystopian imagery, the greater the people's fear and the more likely they are to be scammed. By pandering to a society in distress with promises they want to hear, con men create an emotional bond with their victims, blinding them to the way they are being manipulated, and making them believe that only they can take care of their needs.

It is easy to recognize that Trump has managed to strike a deep and responsive chord with angry and alienated voters – people who had become disenchanted and dissatisfied with the government. His support base is white working-class voters, people who feel especially vulnerable due to their limited psychological and financial resources and the disappearance of their jobs. Trump knows how to speak their language. He seduces them with simplistic slogans that draw in the crowds and rally their emotions. Categorizing people into a variety of enemy camps enables him to suggest simplistic solutions such as building a wall and spares him from confronting and working with a much more complex worldview. But throughout his election campaign, and since he has been in office, Trump has left a trail alienating Muslims, Native Americans, African-Americans, Hispanics, Jews, war heroes, the bereaved family members of US servicemen and women, the disabled, women – and even babies. And if that's not enough, he has also not refrained from blanket insults of whole nations, including Mexicans, Swedes, Canadians, and Australians. Trump looks like the ugly American on steroids. But one thing is sure: given his unpredictable behavior, he – and by extension the US – can no longer be trusted by friends or enemies alike.

But although members of Trump's original constituency are still mesmerized by his con game, US citizens, and large groups of people from around the world, are increasingly appalled by his behavior. His overt racism, misogyny, and crude nationalism run counter to the values they value. Unfortunately, encouraged by his behavior, extremist groups in countries that have been affected by waves of immigration, and have been hurt by globalized free trade, are beginning to mimic him. There is no doubt that Trump's election has emboldened some of the more right-wing demagogues in Europe.

As a highly effective con man, Trump has never stopped telling people that he knows how to make America great again, and, as a malignant narcissist, he uses fear to bring out the worst in people. In addition, he plays up the blame game, creating splits between his supporters and supporters of the supposed failed politicians of the establishment. This divisiveness gives him power. In this fractal confusion, he presents himself as the autocrat who has all the answers.

From a branding point of view, Trump's aim to "Make America Great Again" is having the opposite effect. Instead of advancing the values that do make America great, it is reinforcing the image of the ugly American. The most powerful person in the world is a man who confabulates and distorts and sends hostile and menacing messages to people around the world. Trump's inner theater is populated by real but many invented enemies. Righteousness and vindictiveness are his beacons. Fear and division drive his dark vision.

Not only has the Trump circus created havoc within the United States, it has also inflicted serious damage to the reputation of America abroad. In an alpha-male display at his presidential inauguration, stating that "From this day forward it is going to be only America first, America first," he sent an alienating shot that echoed around the world. Trump's dark *Weltanschauung*, full of fear, prejudice, and mistrust, is compromising America's ability to set the example on a world stage.

Given Trump' self-imposed, limiting views, senior government officials and top executives of corporations in countries around the world are scrambling to figure out how to deal with this unpredictable, psychologically challenged leader. But to understand what makes him tick, they may need to undertake a crash course in personality disorders.

Trump (who has a non-systemic view of how things are connected) doesn't realize that he cannot run his administration the same way as he has dealt (not very successfully) with people in his business ventures. He seems unwilling to recognize that he lives in an interconnected, networked world where global trade not only spurs economic growth but also creates international bridges. A superpower like the United States has a responsibility to be a role model to the rest of the world. Its actions, or lack of action, have enormous impact. Trump's unholy adherence to the behaviors described in *The Ugly American* and *Nineteen Eighty-Four* is everything that the US historically has not stood for. It will *not* make America great again. Increasingly, Trump's presidency is becoming a huge betrayal of the democratic values on which the US has been built – universal values that uphold other people's rights, based on egalitarian judicial and educational systems, and the ability to provide economic opportunities for all. America's greatness is based on its appreciation of the creative abilities of its immigrant workers, religious freedom, a free press, equal opportunities, upward mobility, an outstanding system of higher education, entrepreneurship, and an unrivaled talent for innovation. America's greatness is exemplified in its ability to engage with people of other nations, not its ability to make a deal. It is the "land of the free" and "the home of the brave" that gave Europe the Marshall Plan, helped establish the United Nations, encouraged countries to decolonize, and stood up to nations that bullied others.

It may be pie-in-the-sky, but we can always hope that Trump will belatedly realize the importance of how to brand America differently. But, given his personality makeup, I view this as so unlikely as to be a miracle. Of course, the real miracle would be his removal from office. Obviously, politically illiterate as he is, he doesn't recognize that populist regimes set the stage for economic decline, or that his behavior and actions are a prescription for littleness. Throughout the world, the leadership of most countries has a lesser view of the United States under Trump.

Many are still struggling with disbelief that he is actually in office. Whatever his popularity at home, it's clear is that his leadership style doesn't help the international perception of the American brand.

Here's a story to illustrate the harm that someone like Trump can do.

One man takes another to the local judge, saying, "This man has spread false rumors about me and done a lot of damage to my business and reputation."

The other man says quickly, "I realize I should apologize for my behavior. So let me go on record as saying that I apologize. I hope you are now satisfied."

"Well," says the first man, "I appreciate your apology, but I'm afraid it comes too late. You can't take back what you said about me or put right the damage your lies have done."

"Nonsense!" the slanderer replies. "I've taken back my words, so the problem is solved. Nothing more to be done."

After listening to this heated discussion, the judge says to the slanderer, "Listen, if you really want to do something about the damage you've caused, come to the town square tomorrow and bring a feather pillow with you."

The next day the slanderer comes to the town square with the pillow and hands it over to the judge. "Tear it open," says the judge, "and swing it round your head."

The feathers fly everywhere.

"Good work," says the judge. "Now go and get all the feathers and bring them back here."

"That's impossible!" says the slanderer. "They're all over the place. The wind's taken most of them away. It'll take me forever."

"Well, exactly," says the judge. "Just like you can't get the feathers back, you can't take your words back. By now, they've been heard all over the world. Be very, very careful what you say."

5

Not All Narcissists Are Created Equal

*I am so clever that sometimes I don't understand a single word of what I
am saying.*
—Oscar Wilde
For the most part people are not curious except about themselves.
—John Steinbeck

Ronald was very pleased with himself. Once again, he had pulled a fast
one. And as had happened many times before, he had gotten away with it.

Ronald's was a dog-eat-dog world; life was all about looking out for
Number 1. Most deals were win-or-lose propositions, and most people
were either winners or losers. And he wasn't willing to be a loser – in fact,
he saw himself as an exceptional dealmaker – so he was conniving and
ruthless. If you didn't take advantage of others, others would take advantage of you. And you better fight for your rights!

But despite his dark worldview, Ronald could present a charming exterior. He liked creating a buzz, creating excitement. He told people what
they wanted to hear, and used exaggeration and embellishment to impress
them – and when that didn't work, he'd try a mix of lies, half-truths, and
obfuscation.

© The Author(s) 2019
M. F. R. Kets de Vries, *Down the Rabbit Hole of Leadership*,
https://doi.org/10.1007/978-3-319-92462-5_5

Often, he marveled at the naivety of his adversaries. Didn't they realize that honoring your agreements was relative? That a contract was nothing more than the beginning of a discussion?

Ronald knew that people accused him of being unscrupulously manipulative. Could he help it that he had a natural sense for how to play people against each other – for being keenly perceptive of his adversaries' Achilles, heels? He *had* to be Machiavellian in the business world. Being otherwise meant being weak. And Ronald hated weakness.

Ronald felt no need to apologize for how well his *modus operandi* had paid off. With a string of successful deals behind him, he had earned a celebrity lifestyle: money, cars, homes, and admiration. All his ex-wives had been very attractive.

Yes, there were haters, who said he was vindictive or untrustworthy, but Ronald felt these criticisms were blatantly unfair. They were plainly rooted in envy of his talent.

Worrisome Encounters

Have you ever met a person like Ronald? And if so, have you ever wondered, "What's that guy all about?"

In 1964, well-known psychoanalyst Erich Fromm first coined the term "malignant narcissism." He described it as a "severe mental sickness" that embodied "the quintessence of evil." Other clinicians joined him in this diagnosis. For example, another psychoanalyst, Otto Kernberg, defined malignant narcissism as "an extreme form of antisocial personality disorder that is manifested in a person who is pathologically grandiose, lacking in conscience and behavioral regulation, and with characteristic demonstrations of joyful cruelty and sadism." Malignant narcissists engage in emotional rape, while denying that they are doing so even when presented with hard evidence.

Having said this, I should stress that any attempt to categorize someone else's motivations and behaviors can be overly simplistic or reductionist. Too often we label people without understanding the context and the dynamic nature of human functioning. At times, however, putting a label on a specific behavior pattern can provide an anchor point, especially with people like Ronald, whose manipulative behavior can be contradictory and confusing. Given the way these types of people victimize and terrorize those who surround them, the rest of us need to know what makes them tick before it is too late.

Clinicians like Fromm and Kernberg agreed that while narcissistic personality disorders are quite common, malignant narcissists are an unusual variant. In more than one way malignant narcissism is a collusion of two personality disorders. It has all the symptoms of the narcissistic personality disorder but in a more extreme form.

The literature on narcissism is mixed. While many people express some narcissistic tendencies, fully-fledged narcissistic personality disorder (NPD) is less common. According to one study, 6.2% of the general population has experienced NPD in their lifetime (the majority men). Other studies have found that this figure may be as high as 10%.[1]

Malignant narcissists are an even smaller segment of society; some research suggests they make up around 4% of the total population. What differentiates the two types is the malignant narcissist's pattern of sadism, or the gratuitous enjoyment of others' pain. A key defining feature of malignant narcissists is their lack of empathy. While common-or-garden narcissists are capable of being callous and abusive, and may purposefully damage other people in pursuit of their own selfish desires (possibly with some regret), malignant narcissists have little or no conscience. They will be seriously callous and abusive, cause deliberate harm to others, and have little or no regret for the damage they cause.

Although malignant narcissists might acknowledge the difference between what society considers "right" and "wrong," the real meaning of these distinctions is lost to them. They don't possess the socializing emotions, such as love, anguish, joy, disgust, shame, and guilt, that guide our relationships with others. They do not experience remorse, and are unable to feel pity or compassion for others.

A side note: if you think this sounds more like sociopathy or psychopathy, you're not altogether wrong. (The words psychopath and sociopath are often used interchangeably. Some argue that psychopaths are born the

---

[1] http://www.apa.org/monitor/2011/02/narcissism.aspx

way they are, while sociopaths are more a product of their environment.) The malignant narcissist and the psychopath are like cousins, although psychopathy is very rare – probably only 1–2% of the population.[2] What differentiates the malignant narcissist from the psychopath is that the latter is not an attention-seeker, and displays more predatory behavior. Generally, psychopaths do not look for attention, and certainly not acceptance (at least not for its own sake). Malignant narcissists are miserable, however, if they don't get attention, and feel very hurt when they are rejected. Furthermore, they display emotions openly, something psychopaths don't bother to do. To psychopaths, attention and acceptance are not goals or ends, just means to an end.

While run-of-the-mill narcissists have a marked sense of entitlement, score low on empathy, and can be exploitative of others, malignant narcissists are much more strongly marked by these negative characteristics. They are short-tempered, thin-skinned, and unable to listen or to accept other people's opinions. However, because of their talent for mimicry, they can beguile people and make favorable first impressions. But in the long term, the people they interact with are less likely to be fooled.

The ability of malignant narcissists to plan has been well documented by Kernberg and others. Planning for the long term can be very boring, and malignant narcissists hate being bored. Unsurprisingly, their behavior is centered on short-term gains. They are masters at seizing opportunities but very poor in thinking through the consequences or next steps. In the long run, because they view the people they associate with as competitors or prey, malignant narcissists undermine the organizations they are involved in.

Many psychiatrists hypothesize that the cause of malignant narcissistic behavior is extreme childhood abuse. Some argue that this kind of behavior has a genetic component, and that childhood traumas can aggravate the symptoms.[3]

The question then becomes how we can deal with malignant narcissists. Can they be cured, or at very least, properly managed? Unfortunately, my psychotherapeutic experience suggests that while malignant narcissists are not as troublesome as real psychopaths, very little can be done.

---

[2] http://citeseerx.ist.psu.edu/viewdoc/download?doi=10.1.1.578.2876&rep=rep1&type=pdf
[3] Kets de Vries (2014).

The primary reason for this is that malignant narcissists are extraordinarily adept at what psychologists call impression management. Skillful shape shifters, they can portray many diverse social faces or personas to manipulate those around them. Attempts to help them can end up badly for the person trying to do the helping. The most likely outcome is further manipulation and harm.

Moreover, when these emotional manipulators are confronted with their wrongdoings, they usually resort to anger, defensiveness, and vindictive rage. They almost never accept responsibility for their own actions. If things turn out badly, it's always someone else's fault. Whatever efforts are made to show them the errors of their ways, they will keep on deceiving and manipulating others to attain their own personal goals. So, if you have no choice but to work with a malignant narcissist, your second-best option is flattery. It will take something out of you, but it's the method most likely to work.

However, your best option is to run, not walk, in the other direction. Remember George Bernard Shaw's comment: "I learned long ago, never to wrestle with a pig. You get dirty, and besides, the pig likes it!"

Here's a sad and cautionary tale. A woman had a very abusive husband who seemed to like nothing better than tormenting her. Completely self-involved, and indifferent to her needs, he was a nightmare to live with. Her life was hell, as every day brought new miseries. Then one day the wife noticed a dramatic change in her husband's attitude. He began to treat her kindly. Totally dumbfounded by his change in behavior she had to ask him what had changed. "Why haven't you been like this from the beginning of our marriage? What has happened to you?"

And her husband said, "Well, I heard a few days ago that people who suffer in this world will earn a place in heaven."

6

Do You Identify with the Aggressor?

*The tendency to aggression is an innate, independent, instinctual disposition
in man. … It constitutes the powerful obstacle to culture.*
—Sigmund Freud
Aggression unopposed becomes a contagious disease.
—Jimmy Carter

Everyone was scared of Derek, a senior VP in an engineering firm. His temper tantrums were legendary. When he felt crossed, he would publicly castigate whoever got in his way. His tendency toward extreme micromanagement made him insufferable. And if this behavior wasn't enough, he kept taking credit for other people's work, which created huge resentment. Unsurprisingly, given his leadership style, his subordinates were perpetually on edge, always wondering when it would be their turn to be his target. Derek's toxic behavior pervaded the whole company and had a seriously negative impact on morale.

Worst of all, Derek's leadership style led to copycat behavior, with some of his key lieutenants mimicking his abusiveness. Like Derek, they developed a knack for terrorizing the people who worked for them. They seemed to have turned into mini versions of their boss.

© The Author(s) 2019
M. F. R. Kets de Vries, *Down the Rabbit Hole of Leadership*,
https://doi.org/10.1007/978-3-319-92462-5_6

This form of copycatting is a psychological behavior pattern known as identification with the aggressor. In painful and extremely stressful situations, people mirror the person who represents the threat. This defensive response is an attempt to conquer their fear by becoming like the person terrorizing them. This dysfunctional behavior is a form of traumatic bonding and is typical of people who find themselves in a weak position. It can even be called a survival strategy – a way of dealing with an overwhelming sense of powerlessness.

Two psychoanalysts introduced this psychological defense mechanism into the literature on child development. Sandor Ferenczi found evidence that children who are terrified by out-of-control adults will "subordinate themselves like automata to the will of the aggressor." And according to Anna Freud, "by impersonating the aggressor… the child transforms himself from the person threatened into the person who makes the threat."

In its mildest form, identification with the aggressor may serve an evolutionary purpose and can be seen as a healthy defense mechanism. It allows people to adjust to situations they perceive as threatening. A similar pattern can be observed in the kinds of games children play. Often, they try to overcome the things they fear – scary animals or monsters – by pretending to be like them. Through play-acting, they transform their anxieties into identifications, and become better equipped to deal with them.

As the profile of Derek shows, chronic identification with the aggressor can lead victims to become aggressors themselves. In particular, children who have been exposed to highly dysfunctional childhood practices are more likely to adopt similar negative behavior patterns as a survival strategy in adulthood. Submission to and compliance with the aggressor becomes their automatic defense position. They are also more likely to regress and resort to these patterns when reminded of traumatic childhood experiences. They turn from victims into victimizers, projecting their feelings of helplessness and trauma onto others.

A troubling element here is that people who resort to identification with the aggressor can lose their sense of who they really are. They end up wearing a mask, feeling compelled to present a false self. Haunted by anxiety, they become hyperattentive to people who intimidate them.

And this hypersensitivity to other people's assertive, threatening behavior will contribute to feelings of dissociation (a sense of detachment from physical and emotional experiences), masochistic behavior patterns, chronic hypervigilance, and other personality distortions.

The universality of identification with the aggressor was famously illustrated by Stanley Milgram's disturbing experiments in the 1960s, in which he assessed the willingness of a group of volunteers from a wide variety of backgrounds to follow instructions to administer increasingly large electric shocks to subjects. His study showed that 65% of participants were ready to inflict the maximum level of pain, obeying the directions of the organizer. (Unknown to the participants, the electric shocks and the pain delivered were simulated.)[1]

Milgram's experiment showed that most of us are all too willing to give up our autonomy when confronted with forceful, strong-armed figures. It's fair to assume that identification with the aggressor (on a smaller scale) operates invisibly but pervasively in the everyday lives of many people. In the company of authoritative people, we put our own thoughts, feelings, perceptions, and judgments aside, and instead, do – and, more importantly, think and feel – as we are expected to.

Stockholm syndrome is an extreme example of identification with the aggressor. This syndrome was introduced into the vocabulary in 1973, following a six-day bank siege in the Swedish capital in which four bank employees were taken hostage and tortured by armed robbers. As a way of surviving the ordeal, the captives established a misplaced form of emotional attachment with their captors.

The case of Patty Hearst and the Symbionese Liberation Army is another example. Although Ms. Hearst was abused and raped by her kidnappers, she identified with their cause and joined the group, even going so far as to take part in one of their bank robberies. At her trial she was found guilty of robbery but her sentence was commuted by US President Jimmy Carter, and she was later pardoned by President Bill Clinton, having been declared a victim of Stockholm syndrome.

So how can we resist the process of identification with the aggressor? Are we all susceptible to regressing in this manner?

---

[1] Milgram (1974).

The first step in breaking a pattern of victimization is the realization that we have fallen into the trap of identifying with the aggressor. But it is usually others who make us see the light. When we defend or rationalize the actions of someone who is mistreating us, we have already fallen into the trap. It takes people who know us well to see and call out that we are engaging in dysfunctional behavior.

The important question is how we digest this feedback when we get it. Are we ready to face the unpleasant truth that we are turning into the aggressor? Will we be able to admit we have fallen under a spell? Will we be prepared to listen to the comments, and reflect on them?

However easily or otherwise we are convinced, freeing ourselves from an identification bond isn't easy. As humans, we have a tendency to love the ties that bind. What's more, people prone to identification with the aggressor will fend off feelings of shame and guilt by resorting to the defence mechanism of denial. Lengthy exposure to an intimidating boss may have affected their personality to the extent that the changes to their behavior endure even after they are out of the boss's orbit. If that's the case, extensive coaching or therapy can help them realize the roots of their behavior. They need to understand that their mirroring derives from a basic human survival strategy and that there are complex psychological dynamics at play. Only by identifying the source of these dynamics will they be able to exert control. Furthermore a strong, general support system of friends and family is key to prevent them from regressing, and repeating the pattern.

Going back to the example of Derek that I started with, was it inevitable that his lieutenants adopted similar behavior patterns? Was behaving like Derek their only survival strategy? Are there other more productive ways of dealing with the Dereks of the world?

Happily, there are. One way to build up immunity against people like Derek is to band together and create a support group. Support groups can provide strength and reassurance, as well as a reality check to prevent members from identifying with the aggressor. Mentors or coaches, inside or outside the organization, can help people vulnerable to victimization to anchor their sense of reality by providing support, encouragement, and constructive criticism. Another proactive measure could be to build up a political network inside the organization, with the ultimate purpose of getting rid of a toxic boss. It's important to let other people in the organization know about the destructive consequences of an intimidating leadership style. If enough people realize the human and financial costs of such behavior, more senior people in the organization would take notice and force a Derek into accountability. While building a political support group, it is wise to document specific incidents of abuse to build a case (if necessary) for possible legal proceedings.

But remember, in the worst-case scenario, it's always possible to walk away. And remember, too, Marcus Aurelius's remark: "The most complete revenge is not to imitate the aggressor."

Here's a short fable with a moral lesson about identification with the aggressor. One day a lion was walking through the bush and met a small dik-dik. As it prepared to attack it, the dik-dik screamed, "Stay away from me! I'm the king of the animals!" The lion stopped, astounded. "Are you out of your mind?" he said. "Don't be ridiculous. You're just a little antelope. You know very well that I am king of the animals." The dik-dik said, "What? You're kidding yourself. Wherever I go, the other animals run away from me, terrified. If you come with me, I'll prove it."

So the lion followed the dik-dik and soon they came upon a group of impala. When the impala saw the lion, they sounded the alarm and fled. Next, they encountered a herd of zebra, which scattered in all directions. And the same thing happened when they met the wildebeest, giraffe, and water buffalo.

The dik-dik turned to the lion, and said: "Seen enough? All the animals flee when they see me. It's as I said: I am the king of the animals."

The lion dropped to its knees in salute. "It's true. I have seen it with my own eyes. Forgive me for trying to attack you, your majesty." And the lion went on its way.

7

The Making of a Bully

Courage is fire, and bullying is smoke.
—Benjamin Disraeli
No one can make you feel inferior without your consent.
—Eleanor Roosevelt

Ted, a senior VP at a large media company, was notorious for constantly interrupting people when they gave presentations and for his habit of publicly intimidating, offending, and humiliating them. His sarcasm was legendary. When someone said something he didn't like, he wasn't averse to yelling at them. And he could get enraged by very trivial things. Working for him was like walking on eggshells. His work habits didn't help. He constantly made seemingly pointless changes to assignments. He also created impossible deadlines – setting people up to fail. Overwork was part of the deal of working for him. Then there were Ted's emails and tweets, many offensive. Unsurprisingly, his way of running the division had a terrible effect on the morale in the company. Many of the people who worked for Ted complained of stress-related problems. There was a high absenteeism rate and a high turnover.

© The Author(s) 2019
M. F. R. Kets de Vries, *Down the Rabbit Hole of Leadership*,
https://doi.org/10.1007/978-3-319-92462-5_7

When we think of bullies, we tend to remember the ones we had to deal with as kids, the ones who bullied us on the school playground. Unfortunately, bullying doesn't end at high school. Some bullies-in-training turn into full-fledged bullies in adulthood. In fact, the world is full of bullies and bullying in the workplace is more common than we think. Sometimes, it's obvious, but often it's very subtle.

Bullying in the workplace can take the form of repeated emotional and even physical abuse. Although there can be a fine line between having a tough boss and dealing with a bully, one essential prerequisite for bullying is the perception of a serious power imbalance. Bullying is a deliberate attempt to manipulate, belittle, control, or undermine someone. It doesn't just happen in face-to-face encounters. Today bullying is even more insidious with the increase in cyber-bullying – bullying through digital means.

Do you suspect you work for a bully? Do you regularly feel intimidated, criticized, and insulted? Have there been occasions when you have been humiliated in front of your colleagues? Have you been called names? Are your efforts constantly being undervalued? Do you dread going to work? And worse, does working for your boss makes you feel sick? If the answer to any of these questions is "yes," you may be working for a bully.

Many organizations have their resident bully, a pushy and manipulative person, happy to terrorize and harass the people who work there. At work, most bullies are in positions of authority, although sometimes colleagues (and even subordinates) are not averse to bullying behavior. The numbers indicate the omnipresence of bullying. For example, a 2017 survey by the US Workplace Bullying Institute assessing the prevalence of "abusive conduct" in the American workplace reported that 19% of adult Americans have experienced abuse; and 37% (including witnesses) have been affected by it.[1] Although most cases go unreported, at least half of the working population experiences some form of bullying at some point in their career. An even larger percentage of people have been a witness to situations of bullying. And as is to be expected, bullying has a dampening effect on the workplace. It has even been called a silent epidemic. What's more, people targeted by a bully experience stress-related health problems including debilitating anxiety, panic attacks, and even clinical depression. Bullying can sometimes even lead to suicide.

---

[1] http://www.workplacebullying.org/wbiresearch/wbi-2017-survey/

The personality of the bully is hard to pin down. There is no such thing as a specific bullying personality. There are many variations. For example, there could be a relationship between bullying and the narcissistic personality disorder, the latter characterized by a perception of being special, entitled to deserving treatment, and an exploitative way of dealing with the world (see Chap. 4). Given bullies' frequent lack of empathy and little or no remorse for their actions, some even ascribe psychopathic characteristics to them. Generally speaking, bullies have an autocratic personality. They have a strong need to control and to dominate others. But why do they behave the way they do?

One explanation for their unpleasant behavior is that bullies are looking for attention. Their behavior can be seen as a form of relating. And even though the attention they receive is negative, it is still attention of a kind. Being noticed, because of their unpleasant behavior, makes them feel important. They like to be perceived as powerful. Envy, resentment, and feeling threatened – given their inner insecurity about their own competence – can also be motives for bullying. Behaving like this is a way to keep any possible rivals down. Bullies have many other troublesome characteristics, including superficial charm, insincerity, a propensity to manipulate, rigidity, stubbornness, and obsessive-compulsive leanings. They often lack compassion, impulse control, and social skills.

The psychologist Carl Jung noted, "Everything that irritates us about others can lead us to an understanding of ourselves." Bullies project their own feelings of vulnerability onto the person they are bullying. They accuse their victims of the exact actions they engage in but deny. But the swagger hides significant weakness. Bullies are very anxious about exposure of their failures or shortcomings. They fear shame and humiliation, so to empower themselves, they demean others. Their shaky self-esteem means that any form of criticism and disrespect of others immediately offends them, contributing to more bully-like behavior.

Like most instances of dysfunctional behavior, the roots of bullying are usually found in a disturbed childhood. Children become bullies by learning such bullying behavior at home. Very often, their role models are parents who are angry, or don't handle conflict well. They may also grow up in a home where there is little warmth and little positive adult attention – where discipline is inconsistent and where people act in an emotionally and physically abusive way. This kind of behavior has an unfortunate effect on the developing child. It hardens. To be perceived as vulnerable has to be prevented at all costs. Furthermore, in such an environment, behaving in a bullying way has no consequences. It becomes the preferred way of relating to each other. By turning the passive into the active – through bullying – children growing up in this way imagine they will have more control over their lives. Through bullying, they compensate in inappropriate and unhealthy ways for the lack of attention they receive at home. As bullies never learn what constitutes appropriate behavior, they are illiterate as far as emotional management is concerned. They also have a poor social perception of situations. They are swift to interpret other people's behavior as hostile when in fact there is no such intent.

As bullying is learned behavior, it should be possible to unlearn it. However, changing bullies' behavior isn't easy, given their love affair with power and domination. It is made more difficult by situations where bullying is an acceptable part of organizational culture. Although high-performance organizations purge bullies, some organizations promote them. In many organizations there is a fair amount of denial, rationalization, and even tacit acceptance of bullying, especially where they are perceived as rainmakers – meaning great profit contributors. From that perspective, bullying may be rewarded as the kind of behavior that ensures company success, ignoring the serious consequences such toxic behavior has for an organization's long-term sustainability. Surveys about workplace bullying suggest that the majority of employers do nothing and resist taking action when bullying behavior is identified.[2] The question is, why?

Even when there is a desire among an organization's leadership to help the bully to change, rather than fire him or her, it will be an uphill challenge. It's difficult to unlearn behavior that has been learned over a long period of time and it's not going to be easy to set up some kind of treatment plan. Of course, having a realistic treatment plan depends on whether bullying or not is a systemic problem in the organization. If there are hidden forces in the organization – social defensive structures – bullies will stay bullies and victims stay victims.

If a treatment plan is put into place, it should be made unambiguously clear to the bully that there will be consequences if his or her behavior

---

[2] http://www.workplacebullying.org/faq/

fails to improve. Unfortunately, bullies do not have a lot of self-insight and have very little understanding of the feelings of others. They are unaware of the negative effects of their behavior and the damage they cause. They don't realize that their behavior is insensitive and inconsiderate or that what they're doing or saying hurts other people.

But if bullies are taken to task by senior management, they must have a sense that all is not well. Hopefully, they realize that something is wrong. Generally speaking, their negative state of mind will not make for a happy life. Some people think that the answer is an executive coach. But coaches have to be careful about the way they deal with bullies. They have to take it one step at a time. Before exploring the underlying dynamics that might explain the bully's dysfunctional behavior, coaches or therapists should start at a surface level, discussing a number of actions that warrant change. For example, they could agree on one negative behavior pattern that needs to be replaced with more positive behavior. Of course, it is advisable to start with behavior that's easier to change. Once one behavior pattern has changed, other seemingly harder to modify behaviors might also change. It's important that bullies learn the impact of their actions on others, and that their behavior has consequences for which they should feel responsible.

Two important challenges for bullies are anger management and impulse control. They need help in learning to manage anger, hurt, frustration, and other strong emotions. They need to find more acceptable outlets to reroute their aggressive impulses. Sport could be an answer. Sport can also encourage the bully to develop a social network, enabling friendship skills. They have to unlearn their dysfunctional behavior, and learn more effective ways of dealing with people. To do this, they need to build on their empathic skills and appreciate how others feel when exposed to their bullying. Role-play, when coach and client take turns in bullying and being bullied, can also be helpful. Bullies need to learn that bullying is for losers. Blowing out other people's candles doesn't make your own shine brighter. Making other people look and feel small is not the route to greatness.

An equally pertinent question is what to do when you are the target of a bully? How can you handle that situation? Of course, the wisest strategy, if possible, is avoidance. But if that's not possible, the challenge is not to play the bullies' game, not to be baited, not to stoop to their level, not to get emotionally hooked. If bullies get no reactions, they might stop playing their games. But if they continue to do so, it's important to set boundaries. Make it clear that their behavior will be documented and that if they don't stop, they will face disciplinary action. When recording their behavior, get the support of co-workers as witnesses. Unfortunately, in many instances, bullying is sustained by the silence of people who witness it but say nothing. But turning a blind eye is another form of bullying. Cyber-bullying may be more insidious compared to more traditional forms of physical and emotional abuse, but conversely it leaves digital records. This documentation can be used to build a case for HR, elaborating how bullying behavior is affecting the work efforts of the people in the organization. When presenting this documentation, it is important to build a business case. It needs to be made clear that however valuable the bully's qualities, he or she will be just too expensive to keep. If you are unlucky enough to be bullied, it's wise to build a support network outside work to support your confidence and resilience. When bullying behavior is encouraged by management, and has become part of the corporate culture, your best strategy is to quit such a toxic environment. As has often been said, people don't leave bad jobs – they leave bad bosses.

Here's a story about bullying. Once upon a time, there was a man whose boss was a bully. Whatever he did, and however hard he worked, it was never good enough. Over and over again, he was berated for the slightest things. Most recently, he had argued with his boss over a business trip. His boss told him that he was wasting company money. Instead of making three separate trips to three different locations, it would be much more efficient to fly from one to another, and spend the weekends in hotels preparing for the next assignment. When the man protested that his wife was not well and needed him, his boss ignored his comments.

Some time later, in the office, his boss suddenly exclaimed, "I feel really sick. Get me a doctor!" The man left immediately and soon reappeared with a doctor and two other people. His boss said, "What are those other two doing here?" The man replied, "You're always telling me to be more efficient and save time and money, so I've brought along a priest and undertaker as well, just in case things don't work out."

8

Are You Addicted to Power?

Nearly all men can stand adversity, but if you want to test a man's character, give him power.
—Commonly attributed to Abraham Lincoln
Power corrupts, but lack of power corrupts absolutely.
—Commonly attributed to Adlai Stevenson

Greg, a high-level executive at a large financial institution, enjoyed the attention, rank, status, control, and recognition that came with the job. Rubbing shoulders with other high-status people gave him a high. He liked it when people deferred to him and wanted to please him. He loved being at the annual meetings of the World Economic Forum in Davos, Switzerland. Being part of that gathering was a real adrenaline boost. It gave him the opportunity to exchange ideas with the kind of people he would otherwise only read about in the media. To Greg, life was all about power and money.

Given all this, and the pleasure Greg drew from his position, it was a real narcissistic injury when he lost his job and things changed dramatically overnight. He grieved for his previous lifestyle. The people with

© The Author(s) 2019
M. F. R. Kets de Vries, *Down the Rabbit Hole of Leadership*,
https://doi.org/10.1007/978-3-319-92462-5_8

whom he used to associate were no longer interested in him. It was as if he had become completely invisible. Being out of power meant being out of the limelight and away from the action. It meant the loss of his social role and the perks that came with it. Greg came to realize that his total involvement in organizational activities had isolated him from real relationships and real connections. It made him wonder whether he had any real friends. Had all his relationships been fair-weather friendships? The dramatic change in his status made him question who he really was, leaving him confused and stressed out.

Greg's troubled mental state was noticeable at home. His relationship with his wife was no longer what it had been. They were like two roommates boarding together. To compensate for what was lacking at home, Greg had a few superficial affairs and one-night stands, but these dalliances didn't give him the satisfaction he craved. His attempts to replace his former frenetic lifestyle by sitting as a non-executive on a few boards didn't give him the same high he had had when he really was in charge. He realized that he had very few inner resources to draw on. He wondered whether he had given away his soul in exchange for recognition, money, and power.

Maybe Greg's experience feels uncomfortably familiar to you. If so how would you answer the following questions?

- Do you like telling other people what to do?
- Do you define yourself in terms of your title and net worth?
- Do you always like to win?
- Do you like the attention and special treatment that comes with your position?
- Do you like to impress other people?

If your answer to these questions is "yes," it suggests you are very attracted to power and the perks that come with it. But if that's the case, don't worry – you're not alone. Many executives would tick the same boxes. You should realize, however, the corrosive effects that come with power. Throughout history, power has had an intoxicating effect on people, creating a world full of power addicts. In the pursuit of power many people destroy themselves.

This brings me to another question – if power is so important to you, how do you think you will react when you no longer have it? Will your reaction be similar to Greg's? Would you be able to handle being out of power? Remember Henry Kissinger's observation that "power is the ultimate aphrodisiac"? Kissinger was a man who knew what he was talking about.

Although being in a leadership position can be very stressful, it has its compensations. As Greg's example suggests, power can come with great highs. But his example also suggests that pursuing power can involve people in a Faustian bargain, leading to compromises that they may regret later. The addiction to power can even lead to self-destructive behavior.

A major theme in J. R. Tolkien's novel *The Lord of the Rings* is the ability of power to alter a person's character. We see how the Ring (which has malevolent power far beyond its ability to confer invisibility) corrupts its bearers. With each use, the hold it has over its bearer increases.

The Ring corrupts Sméagol (a major character in the saga), who gradually devolves into another personage. Transformed into Gollum, he shows personality traits ranging from withdrawal and isolation to suspicion and anger, behavior patterns that eventually lead to his demise. And even Frodo, the hero of the story, shows signs of addiction, being ultimately unable to relinquish the Ring of his own accord.

To most people, power means having control. Given this preoccupation, we can hypothesize that people who strive for power are trying to overcome feelings of powerlessness. This can be interpreted as a way of compensating for feelings of inner insecurity – a defence against early feelings of inadequacy, weakness, fear, being unlovable or unloved, and feeling worthless. Thus, the wish to have power over others is often weakness disguised as strength.

Many of the world's most powerful people fit into this scenario. Many of them felt neglected or powerless when they were young. Having been subjected to extreme forms of domination as children, their striving to dominate can be viewed as the solution to feelings of extreme submission. Given their early experiences of powerlessness, they are ready to do anything to ensure that they will never be in such a situation again. In particular, the psychiatrist Alfred Adler elaborated how people struggling to overcome actual or felt inferiorities become obsessed by the pursuit of power.

The pursuit of power may have a neurochemical component as well as a developmental explanation. Having power over others has an intoxicating effect. It increases the production of testosterone. But testosterone (the neurotransmitter responsible for producing feelings of pleasure) and its by-products have an addictive quality, because they increase the supply of dopamine in a part of the brain's reward system. As this neurotransmitter is released during pleasurable moments or situations, the good feelings it provides encourage people to seek such a desirable activity over and over again. The dopamine rush that comes from having power explains its addictive quality. But while this desire for dopamine can stimulate the brain to engage in constructive experiences, it also can lead to socially unacceptable behaviors, such as substance abuse, promiscuity, or gambling.

Like many other addicts, people in positions of power try at all costs to maintain the highs they get from playing power games. However, too much power (implying an excess of dopamine production) has an effect on cognitive and emotional functioning. It can make people less empathic, hubristic, and impulsive, leading to gross errors of judgment and imperviousness to risk. Eventually, people with too much power can lose their sense of reality and their moral bearings. They may engage in ethically challenging behavior. As they become addicted to power their inner voice of reason may stop working and before they know it, they begin to live in an echo chamber, believing their own propaganda, and imagining that they are infallible.

Power attracts the worst and corrupts the best. Looking at the world around us, we see that having too much power is a dangerous thing. No wonder – given the corrosive influence of power – that society's demands for moral authority and character increase as the importance of a leadership position increases. Power imposes responsibility.

Unfortunately, given the addictive qualities of power, no individual is wise or good enough to be trusted with too much of it. Attempts at combining wisdom and power have seldom succeeded. The greater the power, the greater the potential for its abuse. It is a rare person who holds power with the intention of relinquishing it. Napoleon Bonaparte certainly didn't fit that description. He once said, "Power is my mistress. I have worked too hard at her conquest to allow anyone to take her away from me." Since power activates the neural reward systems in the brain, people in positions of unchecked power lack the self-awareness required to let it go. They will not abandon it willingly. To quote Abraham Lincoln, "Nearly all men can stand adversity, but if you want to test a man's character, give him power!" Power turns the strongest heads.

So, given what we know about power's addictive nature, in situations where leaders hold a great deal of power, we shouldn't expect leadership transition to be a smooth process. Getting someone to let go of their fix will be uphill work. Most people (and Greg is a good example) find it extremely hard to quit a powerful position. The world is full of examples demonstrating how difficult it is for leaders to let go. There are too many presidents for life. Checks and balances need to be put into place to prevent the abuse of power.

In democracies, the separation of judicial and executive powers, and the free press, all have one essential purpose – to reduce the chance of political leaders turning into power addicts. Business organizations, however, face an even greater challenge. The typical organizational design of most corporations doesn't create democratic institutions. On the contrary, in most corporations, power is concentrated at the top, making its leadership vulnerable to the intoxication of power.

The consequences of this top-down organizational design are there for all to see. The world of business leaders is full of high drama. For example, we find CEOs going on irresponsible M&A adventures that rarely benefit the organization. Other leaders contributed to the catastrophic financial meltdown of the late 2000s, as senior bankers and other masters of the universe made massive bets on derivatives. The sense of entitlement felt by top management is reflected in their excessive compensation packages (see Chap. 11). And I could go on and on.

Institutional measures need to be put into place to prevent the abuse of power in the world of business, as in politics. We have the traditional countervailing powers in the form of the print and digital media, trade unions, citizens' organizations, and, in certain countries, workers' councils, to offset top-heavy organizational designs. Deploying a 360-degree leadership feedback system, or organizational culture audits, can help identify potential areas of power intoxication. But apart from these, the most helpful counterforce would be the existence of an organizational culture where people have a healthy disrespect for their bosses, have voice, can speak their mind, and keep the feet of the people in power firmly on the ground.

Of course, the best people to have in power are those who don't really want it. But even where that's the case, we should ask ourselves whether they will be able to protect their sanity if power is thrust upon them. Which brings me to the sword of Damocles.

Dionysius, King of Syracuse, was surrounded by enemies and under constant threat of assassination. It was said that he slept in a bedroom surrounded by a moat and only his daughters were allowed to shave him.

One day a court flatterer named Damocles was showering Dionysius with compliments, exclaiming how blissful his life must be, and how much he envied the king's wealth, power, and happiness. Dionysius suggested that, if he wanted, he could have a taste of what it meant to be king. Excitedly, Damocles took him up on the offer. Dionysius motioned him on a golden couch, and sent a stream of servants to wait on him. They brought him the most delicious food and wine, and bathed him with expensive lotions and perfumes. Damocles could hardly believe his luck. But as he lay back on the golden couch, he looked up and saw above him, positioned just over his heart, a razor-sharp sword hanging from the ceiling by a single thread of horsehair. Leaping from the couch, he asked Dionysius to excuse him, but he would prefer to forgo the king's privileges. Dionysius had found a dramatic way to convey the high price that comes with great power. A ruler's life may appear glorious, but it is filled with uncertainty and danger.

9

Mission (Im)possible: Dealing with Narcissistic Executives

Self-love forever creeps out, like a snake, to sting anything which happens …
to stumble upon it.
—Lord Byron
Narcissistic people are always struggling with the fact that the rest of the
world doesn't revolve around them.
—Anon

George, a senior executive of a large Internet provider, was a participant in one of my multi-modular leadership development programs. Although a very talented individual, within the group he was looked at as a bit of a nuisance. He tended to monopolize conversations, and appeared to be a know-all, whatever the topic. He was in love with his own voice, and loved being on stage extolling his accomplishments. Everyone agreed he was not a good listener. Whenever someone else spoke, he quickly grew impatient, and tried to change the topic to something he was more interested in. He alienated himself further from the others with his habit of devaluating others while overemphasizing his own successes. George made it quite clear to the other participants that he considered himself superior to most people. I wasn't the least bit

© The Author(s) 2019
M. F. R. Kets de Vries, *Down the Rabbit Hole of Leadership*,
https://doi.org/10.1007/978-3-319-92462-5_9

surprised that most members of the group disliked George and found it very difficult to deal with him.

Among senior managers, the personality type most frequently encountered in organizations is the narcissistic one (see Chap. 4). It often seems as if having a narcissistic disposition – grandiose, self-promoting, larger than life – is a prerequisite for reaching the higher organizational echelons. But this personality makeup has its drawbacks. Although the drive and ambitions of narcissistic people can be very effective in moving organizations forward, the combination of their narcissistic disposition and their influential position (symbolically and otherwise) can go to their heads. Excessive narcissistic behavior can create havoc and lead to organizational breakdown.

Like the Narcissus of Greek myth, narcissistic individuals are self-absorbed and see themselves as the center of the universe. Many narcissists are very manipulative and demanding. When it suits them, they take advantage of others to serve their own needs. Driven by envy, they always strive to win, whatever the cost of doing so. Like George, they come across as conceited, boastful, and pretentious. As I described in Chap. 4, their inner world is populated with fantasies of unlimited success, power, and brilliance. They exaggerate their achievements and denigrate others' success. They see themselves as special, and only associate with other special or high-status people. They also have a strong sense of entitlement. When they don't receive the special treatment they believe they deserve, they become impatient or angry. Given their self-serving mindset, it's difficult for them to recognize or identify with the feelings and needs of others. Empathy doesn't come naturally to them.

Because narcissists are quite thin-skinned, they have difficulty handling criticism. Negative comments evoke secret feelings of insecurity, shame, vulnerability, and humiliation. They are quick to feel hurt. As a countermeasure, they react with rage or contempt, trying to belittle the other person, behaviors that make them feel superior. Although narcissists may give an impression of high self-esteem, the opposite is often the case. Underneath the confident exterior, they are troubled by a deep sense of insecurity. Their bravado is a heroic effort to compensate for their profound vulnerability.

Like most psychological problems, there is no one single definitive cause for a narcissistic disposition. Various biological, psychological, and environmental risk factors contribute to its development. One of the early contributing factors to it is inconsistent or unreliable parental care, neglect and abuse, or overindulgence by parents, peers, and family members. And narcissism breeds narcissism. Growing up in a narcissistic family doesn't do much for emotional connectedness. Given the experiences of their youth, budding narcissists end up without a strong and secure sense of self, focus solely on their own abilities and achievements, and exaggerate them. They become unreceptive to the presence and needs of others.

People in the helping professions have always found it difficult to deal with narcissistic people because of their strong defenses. Narcissists refuse to acknowledge that they have a problem. Why would they ask for help when they think that they are better than anybody else? How can they learn from their mistakes, if they can't admit they ever make any? Narcissistic individuals have very little idea of the negative effects their behavior has on others, nor how their behavior impairs their personal, professional, or other areas of functioning. The people in closest contact with narcissists, and who suffer most of the consequences, are most likely to recognize that there is a problem. Often, however, they are brainwashed into feelings of inadequacy by the narcissists they have to deal with. Trying to make sense of the crazy, can make you crazy as well.

Even if narcissists do have inklings that they have issues, asking for help conflicts with their self-image of power and perfection. Only when their way of relating to others starts to significantly interfere with or impact their life – such as divorce, poor relationships with their children, or being fired – will they consider that something needs to be done. Awareness and acceptance of a problem is a giant step forward in resolving their affliction.

Many forms of intervention have been tried with narcissistic individuals. Typically, because narcissism is a deeply rooted personality trait, treatment involves a long-term intervention. It takes time to help someone better understand their behaviors, moods, and disruptive thoughts, overcome a poor sense of self-esteem and limited self-awareness, and to internalize more realistic expectations of themselves and others. There is no known medication or magic pill to treat narcissistic personality disorders. (Although I should note here that people with this disorder may also be living with depression and anxiety issues, which may warrant medication.)

Given the difficulties in curing narcissistically inclined people, I have learned from my experience in running leadership workshops that using a specific type of group intervention methodology can offer very promising results (see Chap. 20). In a group setting, here-and-now dysfunctional acting out becomes more noticeable, and more discussable. Operating in a group, the focus of attention shifts from the facilitator to group peers. For narcissists, feedback from their peers is often more acceptable than feedback from the group facilitator. Some of their fellow group members may be important enough to warrant their attention. Also, within a group setting, disturbing regressive reactions (narcissistic forms of acting out such as hogging the conversation) are more controllable, creating a more constructive ambiance for dealing with narcissistic behavior.

If the group facilitator can create a safe, playful transitional space, it can become an environment where people with a narcissistic disposition learn to develop trust, explore boundaries, and accept feedback, while increasing self-awareness. And if the dynamics of the group are facilitated effectively, the narcissist's view of him or herself will be revealed, mirrored, challenged, and perhaps modified. In this context, the narcissist's peers will be able to constructively confront problematic behavior while simultaneously offering understanding. Pressure from peer group members will push the narcissist to adapt to the group's norms. Group peers take on the role of enforcers who encourage the narcissist to listen and empathize with others.

Returning to George, throughout the course of the leadership development seminar sessions, I was very careful not to confront him too forcefully when he acted inappropriately. When necessary, I would empathize with George when he showed surprise and hurt by the feedback from his peers. At the same time, I empowered his peers to resist his way of dominating conversations and make him realize that he didn't always need to be the smartest kid in the room. Also, his peers made it quite clear to him that they each had their own needs and the right to be heard. As time went by, due to the interventions of the members of the peer group, George slowly learned to empathize with others. As he practiced listening, he learned from their experiences. He also discovered that constructive criticism from the others could be helpful, not cause total devastation to his self-esteem.

Over time, George opened up and became more trusting of others. He learned to talk about his own needs and feelings, and why he behaved the way he did. He also came to realize the inappropriateness of many of his expectations and that the world didn't revolve around him alone. He began to internalize some of the behavior patterns of the others, which he discovered were more effective at dealing with life's challenges.

Of course, dealing with narcissists will always be a challenge, in a group setting or otherwise. Some narcissistic individuals cannot tolerate the pressure from the group. They are unable to deal with critical peer feedback, and some drop out. Another danger is that other members of the group will drop out, tired of the way narcissists monopolize discussions. They can find dealing with the narcissist's sense of entitlement, lack of empathy, and need to feel special, too much for them.

I should explain that George didn't enter the leadership development program because he felt that he needed to do something about his narcissistic behavior. As far as I could work out, he joined to hone his leadership skills – and, I suspected, to find out whether others realized how glorious an executive he was. Whatever expectations he brought to the program, the results turned out to be quite different. George stopped using attention as an analgesic, having come to recognize the very dangerous addiction to needing to feel significant. Instead of glory, he found reality.

There is an old, animalistic moral tale that illustrates the dangers of dealing with a narcissist. A tiger, a jackal, and a wild boar entered into an agreement to help each other hunt. After he killed a deer, the lion asked the wild boar to divide the meat. The boar divided the carcass very carefully into three equal shares then offered his partners their choice of portions. Instead of acknowledging the fairness of the boar's work, the tiger flew into a rage, and killed and devoured the wild boar. Having polished it off, he asked the jackal to divide the meat once more. Very carefully, the jackal piled up nearly all the meat in a heap for the tiger, and left a minuscule portion for himself.

Very pleased, the tiger said, "Who taught you to be such a good mathematician? You really know how to give everyone his fair share."

The jackal replied, "I learned it from the boar. He taught me how to do it."

10

Developing Leaders Through Adversity

That which does not kill us makes us stronger.
—Friedrich Nietzsche
One who gains strength by overcoming obstacles possesses the only strength
which can overcome adversity.
—Albert Schweitzer

One of the most remarkable pieces of literature known to humankind is the *Book of Job*, written in the period between the seventh and fourth century BCE. The French novelist Victor Hugo once said that if all the world's literary works were to be destroyed, and he could save but one, it would be *The Book of Job*. Not only is Job's tale a narrative on how to deal with adversity, it's also is a moral tale of courage, and of leadership as a force for good.

The tale goes as follows. In ancient times, there lived a prosperous man named Job. He is described as a man of character and moral integrity. Blameless and upstanding, he always strove to please God and avoid evil. His wealth was coupled with wisdom and integrity. Job remained humble amid his good fortune, was concerned about the plight of the poor, weak and helpless, and worked to serve others. Satan, however, was sceptical of

© The Author(s) 2019
M. F. R. Kets de Vries, *Down the Rabbit Hole of Leadership*,
https://doi.org/10.1007/978-3-319-92462-5_10

Job's (untested) moral character. He was convinced that humankind was driven solely by materialism and self-interest. Satan believed that Job only kept his faith because so many good things had happened to him. Take everything away from him and his real character would emerge. Satan's challenge to God was that if Job were no longer under God's protection – if he lost everything he had – he would curse the Lord. The Lord, however, responded that there was no one like Job on Earth: he was a steadfast, blameless, and upright man.

God, to demonstrate his faith in Job, gave Satan permission to strip him of all possessions. Job's cattle were stolen, his servants killed, and his house destroyed by a tornado, killing all his children. And if those were not misfortunes enough, Job was also afflicted with leprosy. But throughout these disastrous experiences Job did not complain. He persevered, and remained steadfast in his belief in himself and in God. His friends tried to sway him, attributing his suffering to evidence of God's displeasure with him. But Job refused to concede, knowing that he had committed no evil deed. He didn't lose hope that, in time, things would come right. As a virtuous man, he would prevail. And that was exactly what happened. All of Job's losses were restored twofold. He had seven more sons and three daughters, gained back twice as much cattle as he had before, and lived to be a very old man, quietly, piously, and happily.

The tale of Job is one of endurance, courage, and character, not of bitterness or vindictiveness. Job shows us the importance of not giving up or giving in – even in the darkest of times. He also demonstrates that adversity can be a great educator. Without adversity, we do not really know what we are all about nor do we appreciate the limits of our character. As C. S. Lewis put it, "Hardships often prepare ordinary people for an extraordinary destiny."

People like Job are role models. They have a deep-rooted faith in systems of meaning. This inner philosophy gives them strength, and helps them to overcome the hardships they face. People like Job also possess a sense of self-efficacy, the belief in their own abilities. Their positive attitude, their ability to regulate emotions, and their capacity to reframe failure as an opportunity for development and growth, help them to overcome whatever obstacle comes their way. Possessing this internal locus of control, they know how to "hang tough" when times are difficult.

To give a different example of this kind of behavior, Winston Churchill, a truly extraordinary leader, delivered a commencement speech on 9 October 1941 to the boys at his old private school, a talk that would take on historical significance due, in part, to its timing and brevity. The great British Prime Minister approached the podium, faced his youthful audience, and said: "Never give in. Never give in. Never, never, never, never – in nothing, great or small, large or petty – never give in, except to convictions of honour and good sense. Never yield to force. Never yield to the apparently overwhelming might of the enemy." Having said this, he walked off the platform without another word. It was a simple message that retains its power to this day.

Nelson Mandela is another great example of a leader who knew how to deal with adversity. He was imprisoned for 27 years (1964–90), for most of that time on Robben Island, spending his nights in a tiny, spartan cell, and his days working under the blistering sun, chipping rocks in limestone quarries. In spite of the indignities inflicted on him, he used his years of imprisonment to further develop his character – and to persist in his belief in human dignity and equality. Like Job and Churchill, he didn't give up. He relentlessly kept pressing for social change. Afterwards, he would comment how William Ernest Henley's poem *Invictus* ("undefeated" in Latin) gave him hope when the future looked very grim. The nineteenth-century poem portrays life not as smooth and flawless but full of troubles. In spite of this, we should stay strong, remain the masters of our faith, unconquered, and look for solutions. By keeping this faith in ourselves, we become "the master of [our] fate" and "the captain of [our] soul," able to face anything in life.

Mandela would recite this poem to himself and the others to maintain faith in the future. It helped him to overcome feelings of helplessness and hopelessness and remain loyal to the cause he believed was right. Through hardship, he tested and revealed his character and became the symbol of freedom and democracy in South Africa and far beyond. As the Roman poet Horace wrote, "Adversity has the effect of eliciting talents, which in prosperous circumstances would have lain dormant."

Leaders like Job, Churchill, and Mandela achieved their fullest potential through adversity. Challenges defined them, strengthened them, and brought out the best in their character. Adversity boosted their effectiveness as leaders. Their example begs the question, however, whether we can simulate life-changing learning experiences to create courageous leaders.

Although character is developed at an early age, experiences later in life also matter. There are ways to develop a moral compass that can be used to make value-based decisions. Many adult experiences – designed, or through serendipity – can contribute to character development. For example, negative experiences at work, like getting unpleasant feedback, being fired, demoted, or passed over for a promotion, can strengthen a person's resilience and ability to manage setbacks. Of course, there are also many positive experiences that can influence character development. Experiences can be designed to mold character, situations in which budding leaders learn to internalize the qualities needed to do an effective job. These are attributes such as self-awareness, self-regulation, a sense of justice, a belief in fair process, a sense of humanity and humility, and – as Job, Churchill, and Mandela demonstrate – courage.

In my work with executives I have learned that a number of interventions can be used to accelerate character development. To start with, senior executives can give their high-potentials tasks that require them to make difficult choices. One way of doing this is to give them meaningful assignments with P&L responsibility. People really learn when they have skin in the game. They will make mistakes, but mistakes are crucial steps toward learning, growing, and improving. The way they deal with these experiences will provide insight into their strengths and weaknesses.

Another great learning experience in the character formation of future leaders is to expose them to multi-party feedback processes. These surveys provide feedback from the people who work and socialize most closely with them – bosses, colleagues, direct reports, friends, and family members – can create tipping points for behavior change. These feedback systems are unsurpassed as tools for learning more about their strengths and weaknesses. Realizing what works, and what doesn't is essential for people in leadership positions, making these multi-party feedback systems great ways to encourage reflection, self-awareness, and character development.

Character building can also take place by shadowing exemplary executives. This is another powerful technique for adult learning whereby a person accompanies, observes, and collaborates with a seasoned executive to learn the best ways of dealing with knotty situations. During shadowing, the actual work of the organization itself becomes the context for learning. In such instances, high-potentials have the opportunity to talk to the people they are shadowing, develop best practice scenarios, and solicit feedback about improving their skills and knowledge. Again, they learn what works and what doesn't work by observing executives doing the right things, and aspiring to develop a similar character.

Finally, leader and character development can be accelerated with the help of executive coaches and mentors. They can guide high-potentials to become more effective in their organizations and help them succeed in new roles that require new skills. By providing knowledge, opinions, and judgment in critical areas, coaches and mentors can help their clients to become more attuned to the soft skills – the communication and relationship skills – required to influence and energize employees. Like 360-degree feedback systems, they can help high-potentials to obtain greater self-awareness about their strengths and weaknesses, and how to deal with adversity.

Given the perfect storm our world is currently experiencing – unstable leaders at the top, chinks in European unity, environmental fears, wars, and financial meltdowns – we need to develop leaders with character, people who can deal with complex and difficult situations, and are forces for good. Today, leaders with the qualities of a Job, Churchill, or Mandela are needed more than ever.

As I discuss in some of the earlier chapters of this book, many of today's leaders are caught up in delusions of grandeur, engage in angry scapegoating, or put damaging spin on wild superstitions. Instead of experiencing moral, value-driven, exemplary leadership, we're witnessing a sad, mega-reality show with clowns in the main roles, as well as walk-on parts.

Let me end with a moral tale. A long, long time ago, an aging king felt that the time would soon come for his son to succeed him, so he sent the young prince to spend time with a sage and learn about the essentials of leadership. When the prince arrived at the sage's modest shelter, the wise man sent him into the forest with instructions to observe and reflect on everything he saw and heard for the next year. When the prince returned 12 months later, he described the sound of the crickets, the buzzing of the mosquitos, the caws of the raven, the cooing of the doves, and the burling of the deer. The sage smiled and told the prince, "Go back to the forest, and listen again." The prince was puzzled, as he thought he had reported everything he had heard. But he did what he was told.

Spending days and nights listening even more carefully, the prince began to hear the sounds behind the sounds: the singing of the wind, the rustling of the leaves, the trickling of the rain, and the sound of the acorns dropping to the ground. When his returned and described what he had heard, the wise man was very pleased. He told him, "You are beginning to hear the unheard. Wise rulers need to hear the sounds that are not communicated, the words that are left unspoken, and the worries that are not being expressed."

Part II

11

A Tale of Two Organizations: Creating Best Places to Work

Excellence is an art won by training and habituation. We do not act rightly because we have virtue or excellence, but we rather have those because we have acted rightly. We are what we repeatedly do. Excellence, then, is not an act but a habit.
—Aristotle

There's no magic formula for a great company culture. The key is just to treat your staff how you would like to be treated.
—Richard Branson

The CEO of XYZ Corporation was a notorious control freak. Symptomatic of his leadership style were the number of so-called internal consultants he kept on the payroll to keep him informed about goings-on in the organization. Many people in the organization described the work environment as a "Darwinian soup" – meaning everyone was out for him- or herself. Information was power, secrecy was the norm, there was no transparency, and teamwork was non-existent. To add to the company's paranoid culture, the CEO had demanded that all his top managers should pre-sign resignation letters. He enjoyed the rank-and-yank environment he had created; in fact, his favorite pastime was ranking his

© The Author(s) 2019
M. F. R. Kets de Vries, *Down the Rabbit Hole of Leadership*,
https://doi.org/10.1007/978-3-319-92462-5_11

subordinates, and woe betide those who found themselves at the bottom of his list. Executives could be fired on the spot for the slightest transgression. At meetings, he frequently subjected his executives to abusive, even profane tirades. During these humiliation sessions, he made it quite clear that all the successes enjoyed by the organization were due to his personal efforts.

At the ZYX Corporation, in contrast, great efforts were made to ensure that everyone in the organization was aligned behind its values, mission, and vision. Top management emphasized the importance of a coaching-oriented, people-centric culture. Employees were proud of the organization as it offered mutual support, promoted trust, and provided them with meaning. People were paid decently, and were given excellent benefits. The CEO encouraged people to speak up, come up with new ideas, and to take risks. Entrepreneurial activities were encouraged. Furthermore, great efforts were made to enable organizational members to maintain a good work-life balance. The company also acted as a responsible corporate citizen to the community and the world at large.

The Authentizotic Organization

As this juxtaposition of the hell and heaven of organizational life illustrates, work environments can range from the awful to the awesome. For many executives the million-dollar question is what can be done to create high-performing, best places to work. Based on many decades of academic experience and consulting with global C-suite executives and organizations, I offer my observations on how to create high-performing organizations in which people can be their best and give their best. Numerous studies have shown that the best places to work have lower voluntary employee turnover than their competitors, are able to recruit the best people, provide top-quality client service, and create innovative products and services – activities that contribute to their overall financial success. Furthermore, such organizations record much higher levels of job satisfaction and engagement. Generally speaking, people who are happy are more committed to their work.

I call these organizations authentizotic, a term I devised by combining two Greek words, *authentikos* and *zootikos*. *Authentikos* means "true to one's values." As a workplace description, it implies an organization characterized by fair processes. This type of workplace emphasizes self-actualization, producing a sense of effectiveness, competency, autonomy, and creativity. The term *zootikos* means "vital to life." In an organizational context, it describes the way in which people are invigorated by their work and are able to find balance, commitment, and completeness, and where the need for exploration – closely associated with cognition and learning – is met.

Authentizotic organizations have what I call C^4 in their DNA: *courageous conversations* embedded within a *coaching culture*. But to create the conditions for authentizotic organizations, a number of ingredients are needed.

Developing Trust

The foundation for developing authentizotic organizations is trust. The creation of a culture of trust, however, starts at the top. Trust is earned when actions meet words. We trust leaders who are forthright, walk the talk, live up to their commitments and promises, set an example, and work with integrity. Consistency in leadership actions is a critical factor in developing trust. This implies following through with what is promised.

Another important factor in developing trust is for leaders to be prepared to show their emotions when appropriate, and demonstrate that they care. Trust, however, is not only affected by the ability to express emotions, but also by the way emotions are conveyed. For example, there are other ways to show displeasure or anger than yelling and losing it – not a way to build trust. The people in charge of an organization also need to have confidence in and appreciate, value, and acknowledge the efforts and contributions of the people they work with. They should make clear that the work of each individual is valued.

Organizational leaders need to listen carefully to what their people have to say. Actively listening to another person means paying attention not only to the story, but also to the underlying meaning of the story, the language used, the tone of voice, and body language. It's equally important to listen to what's *not* being said. Furthermore, the leaders of the organization should be sufficiently psychologically secure to admit that they don't have all the answers.

Trusted executives make a great effort to invite the people that work for them to participate in expressing their opinions – to have voice. They make it clear that people can disagree, and that disagreement is part of the creative process. They present failure as great learning opportunities, while setting clear boundaries of what is acceptable and unacceptable behavior. Just as they do in childhood, such boundaries help create feelings of safety – only when people feel safe will they feel comfortable about speaking up in an organizational setting.

The Clinical Paradigm: A Well-Tested Change Methodology

With these parameters in mind, how can leaders create an organization where people give their best? To enable this, I have designed a well-tested intervention method to create a coaching culture. It's a methodology that helps overcome people's fear of the negative consequences of having courageous conversations – to talk about matters that *really* influence the effectiveness of the organization. This intervention technique builds trust, helps minimize fears of self-exposure, deals with concerns about reciprocity in dealing with sensitive issues (or the lack of it), and deters lingering paranoid reactions.

The conceptual framework underlying this intervention method is the clinical paradigm – the psychodynamic-systemic lens through which we can explore people's inner theater and underlying motivations. The clinical paradigm allows us to explore phenomena that lie beneath our consciousness, and adds a deeper and more nuanced understanding to intra-personal, interpersonal, group, and organizational behavior. Through it, we discover an inner world of fantasy, dreams, and daydreams, all representing forces that contribute to the external reality of decisions, actions, and interactions.

The Clinical Paradigm in Action

The beginning of personal and organizational change starts with an honest look at what holds people back in the organization. One way to identify key developmental areas is through the use of multi-party feedback questionnaires that show the gap between self-perception and the perception of others. If done well, the feedback (preferably shared in a group setting) provides a more rounded portrait of the individual in the organizational setting, an assessment that can have a deep emotional impact. It creates openings for how the organization and its people can change for the better. In addition, ice-breaking activities that touch on deeply felt emotional issues can also help create the kind of transitional space that enable people to "play." From my own experiences with thousands of executives, more can be learned about the others in short periods of play in a group setting, than in hours of presentations. Play unleashes the opportunity to start conversations that really matter – conversations that contribute to change. Group members find themselves able and willing to discuss the otherwise undiscussable.

Another foray into illuminating cathartic experiences is through the process of narration. Being able to tell our personal story to a group of people who listen in a respectful manner has a strong emotional impact. Talking about the things that bother us provides an opportunity to re-experience and transform deeply troubling or repetitive life themes, helping us to better understand why certain psychological issues keep holding us back and why we persist in dysfunctional behavioral patterns that have a negative effect on the organization.

Furthermore, while listening to other people's life stories, we may realize that we are not alone in our confusion. We may come to understand that others, too, struggle with similar problems. This mutual identification with specific problems offers many opportunities to discuss alternative ways of dealing with them. In addition, in the process of giving each other mutual support, all the participants become part of a real, supportive community.

To get the best out of people, courageous explorations and conversations need to be part of organizational culture. The intervention method I describe here will create a culture that reflects the realities of its people.

Courageous conversations can be very contagious, starting with individuals, and then moving through teams, and more broadly throughout the organization. Eventually, this constructive contamination will spread and become integrated into the culture of the organization so that it becomes a place of work that gives meaning and purpose, a place that has the C^4 in its DNA. A very good sign that you are getting things right is when you are being copied – after all, imitation is said to be the highest form of flattery.

So where do you start the process of creating an authentizotic organization? Here's a parable I first read many, many years ago.

"When I was young," said the wise man, "I was desperate to change the world. But everybody I talked to discouraged me. They even suggested there was something wrong with me. Faced with their negative reactions, I was at a loss what to do.

When I was a bit older, I realized that I had set my goals too high – I wanted to do too much. So I decided a better alternative was to try to change my family. But although I really tried, my family didn't seem to be interested.

And now I'm an old man, I realize that I was wrong in trying to change the world, and in trying to change my family. With hindsight, I see that I should have started with myself. If I had been able to change myself, who knows, there might have been a chance to change my family. And if I had been able to do that, it might have been the first step toward making the world a better place."

12

The CEO Mega-Pay Bonanza

There are three faithful friends—an old wife, an old dog, and ready money.
—Benjamin Franklin
The salary of the chief executive of a large corporation is not a market award for achievement. It is frequently in the nature of a warm personal gesture by the individual to himself.
—John Kenneth Galbraith

Alas, what terrible news! According to the most recent report from the Economic Policy Institute, the average CEO-to-worker pay ratio in the U.S. has gone down from 286:1 (in 2015) to 271:1 (in 2016).[1] To many top executives, this disappointing number is far from the peak of 383:1 it reached in 2000. But in spite of this bad news, it's encouraging to know that most CEOs will not receive a pauper's wage.

Looking at these mega-figures, it appears that nobody has heeded the warnings of management sage Peter Drucker, who noted that the proper ratio between a chief executive's pay and that of the average worker

---

[1] http://www.epi.org/publication/ceo-pay-remains-high-relative-to-the-pay-of-typical-workers-and-high-wage-earners/

© The Author(s) 2019
M. F. R. Kets de Vries, *Down the Rabbit Hole of Leadership*,
https://doi.org/10.1007/978-3-319-92462-5_12

should be around 20:1 (which it was in 1965). Drucker believed that larger discrepancies in pay ratio would bring about problems of morale within the workforce. As things stand now, however, many CEOs earn more in one workday than the average worker makes in an entire year. But while CEO pay has sky-rocketed, the average wage of workers has remained static.

Do CEOs Earn Their Pay?

Some would contend that exorbitant CEO compensation merely reflects market demands for a CEO's unique skills. They argue that as the modern corporation grows in size and complexity, reaching the Olympian heights of the CEO position requires tremendous investment, in terms of stamina, political savvy, experience, and competence. Talented CEOs – like star athletes or actors – are considered rarities possessing the scarce leadership skills needed to survive in today's highly competitive, global marketplace. They deserve these high levels of compensation, given the enormous pressures they are under to create exceptional results for the corporation, and the services they provide to society through job creation.

Although these arguments may sound convincing to some, these extremely high CEO compensation packages continue to be problematic. They overemphasize the impact of a single individual and undervalue the contributions of other employees to the success of a company. Mega-pay contributes to the cult of the CEO as the key contributor while discounting the impact of a team culture and distributed leadership. There are studies that show that companies with high CEO-to-worker pay ratios have lower shareholder returns than companies with lower ratios.[2]

These contradictory observations raise the question whether CEOs really deserve their mega-pay? Certain myths contribute to these extremely high CEO compensation packages.

---

[2] http://ctwinvestmentgroup.com/wp-content/uploads/2014/02/CtW-Investment-Group-comment-letter-20131125.pdf

Myth 1: CEOs need high pay to motivate them to exceptional performance

As far as sense-making is concerned, a frequently heard argument in favor of outsized compensation packages is that CEOs will not work so hard if they are not paid so well. For the benefit of the organization, it's essential to motivate them to exceptional performance by offering them super-generous incentive packages.

Reality: High-achieving CEOs work hard whatever they are paid

When we look a bit more closely at this reason, it turns out to be wide open to question. Our understanding of human motivation suggests the kinds of people interested in the corporate game tend to be high-achievers. Most CEO-types fall into this category. From my experience working with these people, they will work hard whatever they are paid.[3] This implies that companies are just throwing money away in giving them such grandiose pay packages, wasting resources that could be used for much better purposes. It's very unlikely that a CEO's pay cut would affect the bottom line.

Myth 2: High CEO compensation reflects market demands for a CEO's unique skills and contribution to the bottom line

Like star athletes or actors, talented CEOs are rare beasts. They have impressive but very scarce leadership skills. They are also very hard to replace. Their generous pay packages merely represent the market forces of supply and demand. If there were an oversupply of people with their unique qualities, these market forces would bring their salaries down.

Reality: CEOs are not that exceptional and it's almost impossible to measure their individual contribution to the bottom line

It may come as a shock but the fact is that most CEOs aren't exceptional. There are very few who have the impact of a Jack Welch, Steve Jobs, Bill Gates, or Jeff Bezos. Although they might like to think that their skills are in short supply, many are quite ordinary, fallible human beings who have only a limited impact on the company they lead. They are not irreplaceable. After all, every year, worldwide, business schools crank out hundreds of thousands of MBAs, many with their sights on a

---

[3] Kets de Vries (2012).

CEO job. Also, focusing solely on the star player in a corporation, however capable, ignores the fact that CEOs can't run their companies on their own. Other people are needed to make it happen. Given the many intangibles in the market place (its various economic upswings and the downswings), it's very hard to determine the exact value a single CEO creates or destroys. A company's success is always the result of a team effort.

The Greed Spiral

To understand why extremely high CEO compensation levels persist and why people continue to buy into the illusion that they are getting their money's worth, we need to look at a number of systemic issues and dynamics that drive the cult of the CEO.

Peer comparisons play a central role in the CEO mega-compensation game. Both members of the compensation committee and prospective CEOs take advantage of the above-average effect. When determining the size of compensation packages, members of the board assume that a prospective CEO must be above average and make remuneration comparisons accordingly. Similarly, when bargaining for a compensation package, no CEO is going to suggest that he or she is below average. All of them want to be paid more than the median.

A further contribution to this above-average inflationary spiral is that board members can fear that they may lose the CEO if they don't offer a salary in the upper quartile of the compensation scale. They might worry that their CEO will be poached by another organization. When these social comparison processes are repeated year after year, they have a dramatic, inflationary effect on compensation packages.

To pour oil on this inflationary fire, many headhunters base their own fee on what the prospective CEO is going to be paid. And as they are operating in a highly irrational, illiquid market with no true pricing mechanism to fully determine what a fair compensation package should look like, they have considerable leeway to jack up the pay package. Most compensation consultants' remunerations are also based on some kind of formula tied to the CEO's pay package. When we combine all these escalating pressures with the fact that many board members often do not really understand the convoluted pay packages designed by these consultants (very often created to justify their fees), it's no wonder that there has been such compensation inflation.

Given the existing pay bonanza, it is fair to say that many CEOs have lost their capacity for fair judgment when making a case for their compensation, acting more like mercenaries than genuine leaders. They are reluctant to recognize that excessive compensation packages have moral implications for everyone else working in their companies. These pay scales transmit the message that the only real contributors are the people at the top. It destroys the sense of community needed to maintain a high-performing organization. It inhibits other people who work in the company from giving their best. The level of inequity might even motivate them to leave. Although some CEOs acknowledge the downsides of exorbitant pay packages, greed is one of the deadly sins and particularly difficult to overcome.

Understanding Greed

As I mentioned before, many CEOs have lost their capacity to judge what's fair in the context of their remuneration package. The question becomes whether many of them realize that greed is a faulty approach to life. It doesn't necessarily leads to happiness. Too much greed often implies that the individual is driven by a sense of deprivation, and experiences an inner void. As with many other disorders, this sense that there is something missing is probably driven by early experiences of missing out. Many overly greedy people are troubled by a defective sense of self. Influenced by their early childhood experiences, they are haunted with the feeling that deep down they are not good enough. To combat their feelings of not living up to standards, they resort to greed, which becomes their way of making up a deficit and feel better about themselves. Money turns into a substitute for the love they felt they had never received. It helps them eliminate feelings of self-doubt, unimportance, insignificance, or lack of worth.

At the same time, greed can be a driver for achievement. Financial success becomes a way to benchmark and keep score. Unfortunately, success may bring only a temporary high that does not last. Another fix is soon required. A greedy person's need for material things will never be satisfied. More and more financial success is needed to bolster their self-esteem, feel good about themselves, and ward off inner feelings of anxiety and depression. But these monetary successes never bring them the peace of mind they strive for. I should make it clear at this point that I am not suggesting that all CEOs are this way inclined; nevertheless, it is quite easy to fall into this pattern of greed. Not much is needed to rationalize their elevated pay packages as quite normal.

Managing the Compensation Game

Unfortunately, we cannot expect the CEO community to be self-policing. As things stand, a number of countervailing pressures are necessary to keep CEO compensation packages within limits.

As a starter, board members need to push back against the above-average effect and not be tempted to make comparisons with outsiders. They should also be wary of excessively complicated compensation schemes that confuse and convolute, making it easier for opportunists to rig the system. Convoluted pay constructions can turn greedy CEOs into financial engineers – focused more on ways to impact the compensations formula than investing in the company's future. Board members need to face the unpleasant truth that compensation packages can be gamed to boost a company's short-term earnings. For example, a focus on stock options and restricted stock grants, instead of salaries, invites manipulation.

Generally, the design of compensation packages needs to be moved away from a short-term orientation to long-term consideration of a company's long-term health, taking all stakeholders into consideration. For example, the German tradition of worker representation on the board generally seems to serve as an antidote to excessive compensation.

Another countervailing force against excessive compensation packages is to make the information about top executive compensation publicly available. Secrecy only contributes to the inflationary spiral. Limits to mega-pay can be set by having the company's shareholders vote on top executives' compensation packages. Shareholder approval should also be sought for the buy back of shares, which is an invitation to compensation manipulation when it is tied to share price. (Buy back often involves pushing the price of the shares up without actually investing in the company's capital, R&D, or workers.[4]) Clawback provisions could also put the brakes on excessive compensation packages tied in to irresponsible risk-taking – again to push back against the temptation to manage for the short-term. It forces executives to return compensation that at a later stage turns out to have been calculated incorrectly.

Another way of pushing back against excessive compensation is taking a hard look at how a company deals with existing tax codes. Compensation behavior is often guided by finding creative ways to maneuver through an existing maze of tax regulations. Here, the government can play an important role in putting on the brakes. For example, implementing higher marginal income tax rates at the very top will have a dampening effect on high compensation packages. In many country jurisdictions, the way stock options are taxed may need to be revisited. Another rather innovative measure to prevent pay packages spiraling out of control is to set high corporate tax rates for firms that have very high ratios of CEO-to-worker compensation.

I am well aware that these recommendations will not be received warmly, as many people view the CEO compensation game as an important bulwark of capitalism. However, the present inflated CEO pay scales make it also a sign of impending rot. While capitalism has many positives, free market ideas in unrestrained forms will have serious dysfunctional societal effects. Unbridled capitalism only contributes to social unrest. It's time for the next generation of CEOs to think more creatively about the challenges corporations face in building sustainable businesses. A good start would be creating fair compensation systems that prevent excessive greed getting the upper hand. They should try to transcend dormant (or not so dormant) tendencies toward greed.

Here's a short moral tale about greed, the red thread that runs through the compensation bonanza. In a far-off land there was a man who had a burning lust for gold. Rising early one morning to shop at the busy

---

[4] https://www.forbes.com/sites/greatspeculations/2016/02/24/how-stock-buybacks-destroy-shareholder-value/#71e6e80e7841; http://www.businessinsider.fr/us/whats-a-buyback-and-why-do-some-investors-hate-them-2016-6/

market, he saw a pile of gold by a moneychanger's stand. Unable to control himself, he grabbed the gold, and ran away as fast as he could. But he didn't get far. The moneylender and other stallholders quickly caught up with him. "What were you thinking of?" they asked. "Why did you take the gold in plain sight of all of us? We could all see what you were doing." The thief was stunned. "Were you all there? I didn't see anyone. The only thing I saw was the gold – only the gold."

13

The Money Delusion

Wealth consists not in having great possessions, but in having few wants.
—Epictetus
A wise person should have money in their head, but not in their heart.
—Jonathan Swift

One of the signature tunes in the famous musical *Cabaret* is "Money," which "makes the world go around." In their burlesque and mocking duet, the singers create the illusion that with money, everything is possible. And they are not alone in this magical thinking. All of us have irrational, magical ideas about what money can do for us, and for others. How many times have you had that "If I won the lottery…" conversation? Clearly, with money, we increase our options. With money, we have a greater freedom of choice. Doors that would previously have been closed might suddenly open up.

Money is one of the strongest drivers in human life, and, from a symbolic point of view, it is also a remarkable human invention. Money is a way of commoditizing human labor in a form that can be stored indefinitely and transferred easily to others in exchange for goods or services.

© The Author(s) 2019
M. F. R. Kets de Vries, *Down the Rabbit Hole of Leadership*,
https://doi.org/10.1007/978-3-319-92462-5_13

Not only does money symbolize economic security, it also represents status, power, love, joy, and more. It is a very versatile resource. Many people use money as a way of keeping score in the game of life. They seem to participate in a winners and losers race whose purpose is the amount of money they make. Those who have lots of money are considered ahead of the game.

Although few people believe that money can buy happiness, many imagine that more money would make them a little happier. Pointedly, they argue that it is better to be miserable and rich than to be miserable and poor – money may not buy you happiness, but it could create a more pleasant form of misery. Unfortunately, and all too often, money comes with a greater price than its face value. When the acquisition and control of money becomes the primary focus, it can contribute to a range of personal and interpersonal problems, including anxiety, depression, paranoia, impotence, impulse spending, gambling, social isolation, suicide, and even murder. Furthermore, the insatiable pursuit of money can turn a decent person into a very unpleasant one. To quote the novelist D. H. Lawrence, "Money poisons you when you've got it, and starves you when you haven't."

The saying goes that you aren't really rich until you have something money can't buy. People obsessed by money tend to forget that they cannot buy happiness, feelings of togetherness, kindness, and all the other more intangible things of life. A Chinese proverb tells us that money can buy you a house but cannot make it a home. Although money can provide access to the best things in life, it can also reduce your ability to enjoy the mundane joys of everyday life.

Paolo, an executive I knew, had a very humble beginning. Through hard work and luck, he became fabulously rich. Unfortunately, after having become wealthy, he changed – and not for the better. Having money seemed to reveal what he was really all about. Money influenced his thoughts and behavior in ways that he was not even aware of and brought with it an increasingly grandiose self-image. Paolo believed that having money gave him the legitimacy to do whatever he wanted. His thoughts and actions toward others changed. Life became a zero-sum-game with winners and losers. Instead of assessing the people he met in terms of their qualities, he classified them according to their wealth. Those with very little money were quickly categorized as total losers. His obsession with money led him to ruthlessly shortchange others, in order to add to his already sizable fortune. It seemed to me that Paolo's rise in fortune corresponded with an equal precipitate descent into the social pitfalls of wealth – such as lack of compassion and empathy, increasing social isolation, and the deterioration of his ethics. Paolo's wealth transformed him from a humble man to one who was arrogant, disruptive, abusive, and openly condescending toward those he viewed as inferior.

Paolo's pursuit of money turned into an addiction: the more money he made, the better he seemed to feel about himself. Some neuroscientists, observing people like Paolo, have suggested that there may be an association between making money and the activation of specific regions of the brain (the sphere where dopamine resides). Dopamine is evolution's motivational reward for doing something that helps us survive, like getting food or reproducing. For Paolo, like other money-obsessed individuals, making money seemed to have a similar effect on his neural circuits, creating a surge of dopamine, resulting in temporary highs. In the longer term, the transient good feelings related to money had negative consequences, however, harming his psychological and physical well-being. His constant striving for wealth and material possessions made him increasingly unhappy. Money issues became a key driver for his divorce and led to estrangement from his children. Eventually, Paolo found himself alone in his large estate, abandoned by the people who had been close to him, and surrounded by servants – a modern Citizen Kane, exemplifying the tragedy of wealth and egotism.

The Psychodynamics of Money

Like other addictive behavior patterns, money disorders are actually symptoms of unfinished business rooted in a troubled past. These unresolved issues manifest themselves as persistent, predictable, often rigid patterns of self-destructive money-oriented behaviors that cause stress, anxiety, interpersonal difficulties, and impairment in major areas of life. Money is recognized as a major source of conflict between couples and within families. It is also one of the most common triggers of divorce and estrangement.

If someone has distorted beliefs about money, whether this takes the form of overspending, underspending, hoarding, serial borrowing, or gambling, we must look back to their early years and explore what money meant in the lives of their parents. How did their parents' behavior influence their life? The attitudes our parents had toward money is highly likely to shape our way of thinking about it. In our inner theater, we all follow a script about money based on what we have observed and were taught in childhood. These early messages influence the attitudes, perceptions and expectations that determine how we deal with money throughout our lives. Money becomes a way of revealing aspects of our inner world through our outer world of possessions and lifestyle.

If concerns about money become problematic, there are a number of questions we should ask ourselves. Did our parents fight about money? Did they use money as a form of control? Or was giving money a way of showing love? If we look deep inside ourselves, does thinking about money summon feelings of worry, guilt, anger, sadness, power, love, or joy? Depending on the responses to these questions, money, and all the things that can be done with money, turns into a measure of self-worth and identity. In contrast, the lack of money contributes to feelings of powerlessness.

The power and meaning we give to our money very much determines how we live our lives. Our ability to integrate our emotional life with material possessions reflects how well we bring our values, beliefs, and desires into our world. But while doing so, it is important to remind ourselves that the most beautiful things in life are not associated with money; they consist of good memories and moments. If we don't value these, they can easily pass us by. Thus, we would do well to remember that money can't buy intangible things like time, happiness, inner peace, integrity, love, character, health, respect, morals, trust, and dignity. Far too often, making money prevents people from creating a truly enriching life. It is also a truism to say that wealth does not consist of having great possessions, but of having few wants. As Gautama Buddha said, "You can only lose what you cling to."

Here's a Zen story that illustrates how money can affect people. A Zen master was deep in prayer when a thief entered his house. Threatening him with a sword, the thief demanded, "Your money or your life." To his surprise, the Zen master responded, "Please don't disturb me – you can see I'm busy praying. Just help yourself to the money in that drawer." And with that the monk resumed his prayers. As the thief was emptying the drawer, the Zen master stopped praying briefly and called out, "Please leave some money because I have to pay some bills tomorrow." The thief obligingly put some back. As the thief was getting ready to leave, the Zen master called out, "Aren't you going to thank me for the money I've given you?" "Thank you," said the thief, and left, now thoroughly confused by the Zen master's behavior.

A few days later, the thief was caught by the police, and confessed to many robberies, including his theft from the Zen master. When the police asked the Zen master to tell his side of the story, he said, "Nothing was stolen. I gave him the money, and he even thanked me for it."

The thief couldn't believe his ears. The unexpected response from his victim made him repent. When he was released from jail, he went to see the Zen master and asked him to accept him as his disciple. He had come to realize that life was about far more than the pursuit of material wealth.

14

Saving a Family Business from Emotional Dysfunction

Let parents bequeath to their children not riches, but the spirit of reverence.
—Plato
All happy families are alike; each unhappy family is unhappy in its own way.
—Leo Tolstoy

What do you think is the best way of dealing with my father? What can I do to convince him that there are better ways of running the business? I have been trying to have him accept my ideas, but he's a poor listener. I really wonder how much he values my opinion. What grates is that he refuses to accept that the world is very different from the time when he started the business. If we – as a family business – are going to survive, we need to do things differently.

These were the disgruntled words of Joe, who had come to me for help on how to manage his father. Joe was the son of an entrepreneur who had successfully created a massive enterprise. But times were changing. The digital world was having a significant effect on the business. But in spite of Joe's pleas for new managerial approaches, his father persisted in his old, familiar ways. To all familiar with the situation, it was very clear that

© The Author(s) 2019
M. F. R. Kets de Vries, *Down the Rabbit Hole of Leadership*,
https://doi.org/10.1007/978-3-319-92462-5_14

their disagreement about how to take the company forward was affecting the business. Moreover, Joe's father had a pervasive habit – when feeling cornered – of playing Joe's brother and two sisters against one another. And Joe needed these kinds of family dynamics like he needed a hole in the head.

Family businesses dominate and are the backbone of many countries' economies. They are also the lifeblood of job creation. Families control 95% of the businesses in Asia, the Middle East, Italy, and Spain. Even in mature economies such as France and Germany, over 80% of companies are family controlled. In the United States (with its strong public stock markets), families control 60–70% of the country's commercial organizations.[1] And this world is full of scions like Joe, who find themselves frustrated by business problems that have become entangled with messy emotional issues.

The old proverb, "From shirtsleeves to shirtsleeves in three generations," reflects current family business statistics. Only three out of 10 family businesses survive into the second generation, and only one out of 10 is handed down to a third. The average lifespan of family firms (after a successful start-up) appears to be 24 years (which coincides with the average time the founder is associated with the company).[2]

While all organizations have to deal with power struggles and conflict, these challenges can be especially tough to manage in family businesses because they're so emotional. Therefore, successfully handing on a family business requires mastery of not only the business, but also of the self. The most persistent complaints I hear are that members of the senior generation refuse to share power with their adult children; that family members are put into management positions for which they are not well qualified; and that it is impossible to have a truly professional relationship with someone in the family (father, mother, uncle, aunt, brother, sister, cousin). And all too often, the power holders in a family business fail to address such problems effectively.

What can we do about this? How can we prevent these interpersonal grudges, misunderstandings, and frustrations from festering to the detriment of the business and the family?

---

[1] http://www.ffi.org/page/globaldatapoints
[2] http://www.economist.com/node/3352686

Focus on the Future

As a way to begin to address the problems, I've found helpful to get powerholder(s) to reflect on scenarios for the future. Do they prefer to act like the French king Louis XIV – "*Après moi le déluge*" – with no regard for what happens after they retire or die? Or would they like to preserve the business for the following generations? If the latter, it will be possible to suggest a number of steps that are needed to ensure continuity. To move forward, however, they need to have the courage to face general business issues (which all companies have to deal with) *and* deal with the complex emotional and relationship issues that underlie family dynamics. In a family business, you need to have both a family that works and a business that works.

Focus on Fair Play

The powerholders in well-functioning family businesses need to demonstrate concern for fairness in their plans and decisions. They must realize that fairness is the cornerstone for trust in whatever they are doing. Actions that are perceived as fair are more likely to be accepted and supported if they follow a number of concrete practices:

1. give everyone voice – create the perception that everybody in the family can make a difference;
2. provide clarity – offer timely and accurate information about family and business issues; and
3. be consistent – apply the rules in the same manner to all members of the family.

In addition, when a family business grows in complexity, the family will do well to re-examine the nature of its participation and engagement as a family group. One important recommendation is to introduce regular family meetings, which (over time) should evolve into a more formal family council. Such a structure can help make people like Joe feel less alone in their efforts to induce change.

Write a Constitution

One of the early essential tasks of these family councils is to help develop and approve a family constitution. In creating an explicit and transparent constitution, family members need to ask themselves, what's the unifying purpose of having a family-controlled business in the first place? What are our values and vision? What is our outlook for the future, for both the family and the business? In my experience, some form of family philanthropy can be a highly effective way of binding families together. Focusing on something that transcends the business – having a mission of service to others beyond securing the financial well-being of the family members – can provide the glue needed to maintain family unity down the generations.

The family constitution should address issues like training and development, how conflicts will be resolved, and decision-making practices. It should also address the critical question of how family members can pursue careers in the family business. Is everyone welcome to work in the company, or are there requirements for specific educational and practical outside experience? Rules of entry and exit should be made clear and explicit, along with how business ownership should be handled and how to ensure fairness and prevent or manage conflict constructively. I have also learned from experience that the pursuit of a successful career for a number of years outside the company (before entering the family firm) does wonders for a family member's sense of self-esteem.

Build a Strong Board

As the company continues to grow, it will need a strong board of directors. Effective boards for family businesses differ from the boards of public companies: they play a critical bridging role with the family council, balancing the needs of both family and corporate system. Effective board members need a deep understanding of the relationship between the family's values and goals and the company's culture. They can also serve as arbiters between family members like Joe and their parents.

Deaf Ears

Of course, these recommendations assume that the family members have a relatively well-balanced mental state, that they are willing to look into themselves, that they are prepared to go beyond blaming other family members for perceived wrongs, and that there is enough good will to enable the family business to flourish. Unfortunately, irrational behavior patterns dominate far too often. And although an astute observer of family dynamics may be able to decipher its rationale – what is going on beneath the surface – the family business may come to a bad end due to archaic conflicts that prove impossible to repair.

Members in a family business might consider asking themselves whether, if they could start from scratch, would they still be working in the family firm? If not (life is not a rehearsal), they would be wise to do something else. But if they love being part of a family business, success for people like Joe will take a lot of courage and much inner soul-searching.

Here's a telling moral tale about the perils of family businesses. The patriarch of a family was close to dying. But he was worried about whether the family business would continue after his death. Despite all his efforts to get them to pull together, his children were always quarreling. Finally, the old man, almost at his wit's end, made a final attempt to show his children the advantages of sticking together. He asked one of his daughters to bring him a bundle of sticks. He handed the bundle to each of his children in turn, and asked them to break it. Although they all tried very hard, none of them succeeded. Then the old man untied the bundle, separated the sticks, and asked his children to break them, which they did very easily.

"My dear children," said the old man, "can you now see the power of sticking together? Sticks in a bundle can't be broken. If you stick together, it will be impossible for anybody to harm you. But if you fall apart, you will be broken, and our business will fall apart too."

Which – sadly – is exactly what happened to Joe's business.

15

The Wise Fool

A fool thinks himself to be wise, but a wise man knows himself to be a fool.
—William Shakespeare
The cleverest of all, in my opinion, is the man who calls himself a fool at least once a month.
—Fyodor Dostoevsky

Andrew was an enigma. His behavior was untraditional, to say the least. It was difficult to figure out what he was all about – whether he was serious, or just clowning around. You never knew what to expect from him. Some thought he was a real pain in the neck. Many felt his mocking behavior and bad jokes were over the top.

It was clear that Andrew loved playing the fool. He liked to challenge the status quo and play the disgruntled contrarian. He was always prepared to think the unthinkable, say the unsayable, and do the undoable. He was a virtuoso at asking seemingly naïve, foolish questions; yet there was often lot of wisdom in what Andrew had to say, and his questions were often difficult to answer. His role as devil's advocate – he used irony, sarcasm, and humor to convey difficult messages – usually led to creative dialog. It challenged others' thinking and logic so that they ended up

© The Author(s) 2019
M. F. R. Kets de Vries, *Down the Rabbit Hole of Leadership*,
https://doi.org/10.1007/978-3-319-92462-5_15

considering creative solutions that wouldn't have entered their mind otherwise.

All of us have heard of court jesters or fools, historically the entertainers in the households of noblemen or monarchs during Medieval and Renaissance times. One of the prime examples is the Fool in Shakespeare's *King Lear*. Like many other fools, Lear's Fool does much more than just provide comic relief. He speaks truth to power and points out things no one else can: he challenges the powerholders, criticizes the king, and is the only person in the king's entourage who has the courage to tell him the way things are. Under his mockery, he creates a serious space for others to reflect and question long-held perceptions of wisdom and truth.

The Fool in *King Lear* is anything but a fool. He is a morosoph, a wise fool. Disguised as mockery or oblique comment, Lear's Fool can say things others hesitate to say, and point out the king's real folly.

George Bernard Shaw once said, "Every despot must have one disloyal subject to keep him sane." Morosophs are important foils for the leader. By virtue of their special position, wise fools have the legitimacy to act irreverently, and in doing so can unmask and call out unpleasant aspects of power. They provide an honest and intelligent critique, a stabilizing force or reality check, of organizational life. They make people laugh at human foibles in general, but at the same time subtly force them to look deeply and personally in the mirror, and question their own reasoning, creating greater awareness of who they are and what is going on. Fools create checks and balances that safeguard leaders from the abuse of power. In some ways, their subversive behavior may turn out to be transformational – as in the case of King Lear, who finally comes to sobering self-realization.

Leaders would do well to surround themselves with people willing to take on the role of the fool. Because power corrupts, leaders should encourage the presence of wise fools as antidotes to the abuse of power. Fools bring the fresh air of reality to leadership behavior. They lessen the chance that leaders will fall victim to hubris. And not being bound to tradition themselves, fools help other people embark on journeys of discovery.

The trickster, a figure related to the fool, is found in many cultures. This archetype might be seen as the fool's mythological counterpart, a bewildering creature that thrives on chaos, thwarts authority, disobeys rules, ignores what is normal or expected, and is an expert at breaking down boundaries. Tricksters are the mythical embodiment of ambiguity, ambivalence, duplicity, contradiction, and paradox. They are boundary-crossers, rule-breakers, and truthtellers, playfully disrupting normal life to arrive at new forms. Like fools, stories about the unconventional behavior of tricksters help us understand what's right and wrong. And like the fool, tricksters function as a countervailing force against the abuse of power. By undermining convention and complacency – creating chaos and unrest – they promote new ideas, and foster new experiences, wisdoms, and insights. They are catalysts for change, agents of creation or destruction, cunning mythical heroes and predatory villains, easily shifting from one mode to the other.

But just as the king's fool was playing with fire when telling the king unpleasant truths, organizational fools and tricksters, like Andrew, tread a fine line in organizational life. They need to realize that there is a limit to the amount of conflict-ridden material leaders (or anyone in a position of power) can tolerate at any given point in time. It's always risky to point out hidden agendas within an organization and to discuss undiscussables. It is an unfortunate truth that, in general, whistle-blowing spells a bad end for individual careers. But in spite of these dangers, organizational fools can help leaders navigate the many pitfalls of leadership and keep them sane. It's a role that requires some finesse: the fool has to provoke those in powerful positions to question their convictions, but be only a marginal presence. Their influence would lose its effect if they came too near to the center of power.

In organizational life, consultants and executive coaches often play the role of the fool. As outsiders they have less to lose. That doesn't mean, however, that fools aren't found inside organizations. Sometimes a senior executive, like Andrew, is prepared to play the part. Some organizations may even have institutionalized positions similar to that of the fool, such as internal consultants, or a kind of in-house ombudsman (following the Scandinavian tradition).

Another way to view fools is as honest and loyal protectors, who allow society to reflect on and laugh at its own complex power relations. They can act as our conscience by helping us to question our perceptions of wisdom and truth and their relationship to everyday experience. Through humor and frank communication, fools and powerholders engage in a form of deep play that deals with fundamental issues of human nature, such as control, rivalry, passivity, and action. Fools provide the opportunity to look humorously (but critically) at our own values and judgments as the powerful socio-cultural structures of power pull, push, and shape our identity. Participating in this form of play contributes to group cohesion and an atmosphere of trust. What's more, it helps the actors work through dysfunctional fantasies, creating a greater sense of reality.

Here's a short tale about how seemingly foolish behavior can be used to defuse a dangerous situation. Once again, a thief breaks into a house in the middle of the night and starts carrying valuable items down to the bottom of the garden. The owner of the house is lying awake upstairs, listening to the noise the thief is making, and wondering what to do. It could be dangerous to confront the burglar. Should she try to stop him? Eventually she gets up, goes downstairs, and starts to help the burglar carry the valuables out of the house and down the garden path. The thief is completely confused by this unlooked-for help and asks the owner what she is doing. "We're moving, aren't we?" says the owner. "I thought I should help you pack." The thief, faced with an apparent madwoman, starts to panic and runs off, leaving all the valuables behind.

16

Down and Out in Beggarland

Never stand begging for that which you have the power to earn.
—Miguel de Cervantes
You cannot hold your head high with your hand out.
—Proverb

There is an apocryphal story about the academic and author C. S. Lewis (of *The Chronicles of Narnia* fame). He and a friend were walking along a street when a beggar approached them asking for money. Lewis's friend ignored the beggar and kept on walking. But Lewis stopped and gave the beggar everything in his wallet. Then he caught up with his friend, who said, "You're crazy. He's only going to spend it all on drink." To which Lewis replied, "What's the difference? I had planned to do the same."

Regularly, on Sundays, I walk from my Parisian apartment to the local market. During this leisurely 15-minute stroll, I usually encounter only two beggars. But recently, I have been struck by the fact that the number has increased to 12. I must admit that their presence makes this walk less leisurely. Every time I meet a beggar, I find myself in a quandary. What should I do? Should or shouldn't I give them money? At the same time, it

© The Author(s) 2019
M. F. R. Kets de Vries, *Down the Rabbit Hole of Leadership*,
https://doi.org/10.1007/978-3-319-92462-5_16

crosses my mind to ask what the government is doing about this boom in begging? And, because that is how my mind works, I start to wonder whether business organizations can do anything to help?

But the immediate conundrum is whether or not to give the beggars something. If I decide to give them nothing, I rationalize my lack of generosity and come up with some (thinly veiled) justification for not giving, such as, are these people just lazy? Are they really in need? If I give money, aren't they just going to spend it on alcohol or drugs? I might remember reports in the media that some beggars belong to begging syndicates that force men, women, and children into a life of organized begging. This particular vein of skepticism is triggered when I see beggars with small children – using them as an emotional prop. I tell myself that if these people put as much energy into finding a job, they wouldn't find themselves in this miserable situation. Finally, if I give them money, I am not merely enabling them to continue on this path? Am I helping or hurting them? However, I also find myself wondering whether giving is a genuine act of generosity and altruism or just a self-serving form of feeling good – a quick and easy way of avoiding a bad conscience with little effort. And giving doesn't really solve the problem. By this time, I've walked past several, uncomfortable either way, whether I've given or not, and my discomfort leads inevitably to the question why there are beggars in the first place.

I realize that my reasoning is based on suppositions and not on factual knowledge of the beggars' situations, making it easier to give nothing and feel much better about saying no. But shouldn't I talk to the beggar instead, ask for his or her story in order to figure out what's going on before deciding whether to give or not?

I'm sure I am not the only person who feels uncomfortable when meeting beggars and deciding to give or not to give. These encounters have an impact on our psyche. They force us to question some of our basic values and motives.

Most world religions reinforce the idea that it is correct to give. The values of *bhiksha* in Hinduism, *zakat* in Islam, and charity in Christianity promote the idea of giving alms. In certain cultures, begging is a way of life. For example, according to Buddhist custom, monks and nuns traditionally live by begging for alms, as did Gautama Buddha, on whose teachings the faith was founded.

What role does the imagery of begging play in our social fabric and our psyche? What do beggars represent? Are they a reflection of our negative identity – something we wish not to be? Are they a portrait of social isolation, desperation and poverty – the lowest depths to which we might sink? Spiritually, could begging be a mirror of an unfulfilled need?

Interestingly, when I ask people their idea of the most catastrophic scenario that could befall them, begging quickly comes to their mind. Beggars occupy a significant place in our inner world. We all seem to have a fear of the beggar-within. Often, when we encounter them in our dreams, beggars stand for trouble. From a symbolical perspective, they have associations with misfortune, social isolation, fear of inadequacy, and concerns about dependency.

These conscious or unconscious associations may have become more frequent as beggars have become increasingly visible in many societies. One reason for the growth in their numbers is the combination of globalization and social and political persecution. For example, in Europe it has become much easier for people to cross borders due to the free movement of labor. A prime example of this is the movement of the Roma or gypsies. Given the discrimination they experience in their home countries, life in the center of Paris is much more attractive than life in a Romanian or Bulgarian village. For these Roma, begging is much more lucrative in Western/Northern European cities than in their countries of origin. This makes begging a mirror of societal problems. Is the individual and society able to accommodate and help people off the streets, or is it (more likely) mere indifference and disregard for the disenfranchised?

There will always be beggars who take advantage of the situation. For example, in 2017, beggars operating in Cambridge in the UK were filmed arriving in the city in a VW Passat, parking on the outskirts, and walking to positions in the town before posing as individuals with disabilities. Cities like Cambridge – with thousands of students and many thousands more tourists – will always be targets of similar begging scams while a living can be made by applying some organization and ingenuity.

However, many of the genuinely homeless and destitute are victims of terrible circumstances. Most have very troubled backgrounds in which mental illness, alcoholism, and drug addiction loom large. Their greater numbers on the streets are partly the result of reforms in many care systems, which have led to the closure of psychiatric hospitals and the discharge of patients. In many instances, people who have been institutionalized for many years are suddenly expected to fend for themselves but are unable to find work because of their mental state, physical disability, or lack of skills. They turn to begging as their only resort.

And begging is much more difficult than it looks. Sitting and sleeping on the streets in all kinds of weather is not for the fainthearted. Encounters with grumpy, resentful people – conflicted about whether or not to give – are not good for morale. The social isolation that comes with sitting at street corners in a filthy and disheveled state adds to the stress. Efforts at cleanliness and hygiene undermine the beggars' activities: looking good is not the best way to solicit handouts. Beggars need to look miserable, dirty, and ill to evoke guilt in passers-by. Begging is a very passive endeavor. It is counterproductive to accost people for money: the usual result of doing so is refusal or a call to the police.

Do Do-Gooders Really Do Good?

But the question still remains: to give or not to give? Should we just let beggars be – begging being a fundamental human right – and conclude that they provide a service in enabling givers to feel good? Is that the answer? But misplaced acts of kindness can also be incredibly foolish. Should we really help turn panhandling into an occupation? By giving we may be spreading a modern plague, as giving may only be a Band-Aid over a far more serious social wound. Shouldn't we make an effort to help beggars in other ways, while accepting that some don't want to be bothered?

Given the self-destructive cycle of begging, we could argue that giving money to beggars may be the least helpful option, as it is only a temporary solution. Our acts of kindness contribute to supporting begging as a way of life. It might make us feel better, but it doesn't tackle the real issue. Giving beggars money might help perpetuate a life without a future. True, giving money can improve an acute situation, but it contributes to making the bigger issue (what most of us consider a meaningful existence) more permanent. Like it or not, giving a token sum and feeling good about ourselves is not likely to create the kind of sustainable support system that beggars need. To make a difference, beggars need more than monetary support. From a systemic, socio-economic perspective, if we stop supporting beggars financially, they are more likely to make an effort to start supporting themselves. It can be hard to distinguish professional beggars from the destitute and desperate. But even if we limit our giving to those we believe are truly in need, our giving could encourage others who are not in need to join the fray and crowd out the genuinely needy.

Sustainable Alternatives

Just as U.N. agencies are seeking a market-based approach to economic development in developing countries, our alms could be better spent contributing to the creation of jobs, incomes, and hope, instead of dependency. Martin Luther King Jr. said, "True compassion is more than flinging a coin to a beggar. It comes to see that an edifice which produces beggars needs restructuring." This does not mean that the initial act of meeting the needs of the poor is unimportant. However, if we feel compelled to give, perhaps the more effective response is to give to charities with a mandate to give beggars food, shelter, access to health services, or help create jobs for them.

Taking this last idea a step further, an important part of a business leader's job is to create meaning for the people who work in their organizations. Although beggars will always be part of a society's fabric, wise leaders are cognizant of the slogan "profit with purpose." They would do well to create opportunities for the people in the organization to help others in a productive and sustainable way. By creating meaningful jobs, they infuse their workforce with the notion that they work for more than just money. Could the business community get together to find creative work-oriented solutions to tackle the beggar explosion?

The philosopher Jean-Jacques Rousseau once said, "When man dies he carries in his clutched hands only that which he has given away." Helping fellow human beings in need is good for the soul. Living by the mantra of paying forward makes us feel better. But we should keep in mind that our charitable actions should always aim for maximum, sustainable impact.

Here's a story that illustrates the moral conundrums of Beggarland. Once upon a time a beggar was sitting at the entrance to a park. A man came up to him and asked why he was there. The beggar said, "I'm enjoying the sunshine, watching the birds, and looking at the people passing by." The man said, "You're just a lazy bum, wasting your time. You should do something with your life." "What do you think I should do?" asked the beggar. The man replied, "You should get up, get yourself a job, and make some money. Saving your money will help you find a wife, marry, have children, earn more money, and become rich." "And then what?" asked the beggar. "Oh," said the man, "then you won't need to work, you can relax, you can take it easy, and enjoy life." The beggar said, "But that's exactly what I'm doing now, without going through all the rigmarole you describe to get there."

17

Don't Let Shame Become a Self-Destructive Spiral

A man must not be without shame, for the shame of being without shame is shamelessness indeed.
—Mencius
Shame is a soul-eating emotion.
—Carl Jung

Steven, the VP Operations of a media company, was asked to give a presentation about their digital transformation program during the annual strategy retreat of its top hundred. As public presentations had never been his forte, Steven spent an extraordinary amount of time preparing for the event. But when it came to his turn, he had an anxiety attack, blanked out, and gave a very bumbling presentation. His audience left with a confused impression of the message he wanted to transmit. The next day, Steven was absent from work, citing health problems. Although he saw a doctor, the prescribed medication did little to change his state of mind. Subsequently, Steven went on extended sick leave. Friends who talked to his wife learned that she was at her wits' end. She didn't know what to do with him. Most of the time Steven sat in his study, staring out of the window, not interested in anything.

© The Author(s) 2019
M. F. R. Kets de Vries, *Down the Rabbit Hole of Leadership*,
https://doi.org/10.1007/978-3-319-92462-5_17

What's going on with Steven? What lies at the source of such an extreme reaction? One possible answer is that he is troubled by an often overlooked, unspeakable set of emotional reactions that arise through seeing the self negatively. It's called shame. Shame is a continuing presence underlying all human relationships. We never name it, nor are we often consciously aware of it. And even when we realize its presence, it takes a lot of courage to talk about shame for fear of being ashamed.

Given the way we react to shame, it shouldn't come as a surprise that the roots of the word derive from an older Proto-Indo-European word, meaning "to cover." To feel ashamed has associations of wanting the earth to swallow us up, or a desperate desire to run away and hide under a rock. The Biblical tale of Adam and Eve's exile from the Garden of Eden clearly illustrates the overwhelming effect of shame. After having eaten the fruit from the Tree of Knowledge, not only did they try to hide from God, they also attempted to cover themselves, ashamed of being naked.

The tale from the Book of Genesis is a key motif in all our experiences involving the shame (and fear) of being exposed to others (or ourselves). It sits at the heart of feelings of low self-esteem, a diminished self-image, a poor self-concept, and the perception of having a deficient bodily physique. And no other effect is more disturbing or destructive to the self. Shame can define who we are. It can also push us down a rabbit hole, as it did to Steven, into an unraveling downward spiral.

Feeling Like Damaged Goods

People who pathologically feel shame tend to internalize and over-personalize everything that happens to them. They cannot see things in perspective. When something goes wrong, they say to themselves, "I'm to blame for what happened; it's entirely my fault." Not only do they demean themselves, they also feel helpless, and don't believe there's anything they can do to change the situation. The strong internal critic inside their head continuously judges and criticizes them, telling them that they are damaged goods, that they are inadequate, inferior, or worthless, that they're not good enough, and that they are deeply flawed.

Deep-seated or excessive feelings of shame can have a profound effect on our psychological well-being and lie at the heart of much psychopathology. Shame is concealed behind guilt, lurks behind anger, and can be disguised as despair and depression. Shame also hides itself behind many addictions and disorders, including depression, anxiety attacks, post-traumatic stress disorder, substance abuse, eating disorders, aggression, and sexual dysfunction. In the direst of cases, shame can even lead to suicide.

As people rarely talk about experiences of shame, it is a difficult emotion to detect, especially as it comes in so many disguises. Generally speaking, in working through the shame experience, we can observe two general strategies: attacking the self or attacking others. Someone experiencing shame often shows reactions of avoidance, defensiveness, and denial. Initially, however, during a shame experience, hostility is directed inward, toward the self ("I'm worthless," "I've never been any good"). Some (like Steven) even go as far as withdrawing from the real world. Alternatively, in an attempt to feel better, some people experiencing shame will strike out, and blame others. Others may compensate for feelings of shame or unworthiness by being exceptionally nice to others, in the hope of improving their feelings of self-worth. Although these various scripts can temporarily help the person feel better, they ultimately make matters worse. Without addressing the source of shame, a self-reinforcing negative feedback loop is enacted through which shame chisels into the core of a person's psyche.

Origins of Shame

Given the pervasiveness of this emotion across ages and cultures, what's the adaptive purpose of shame? From an evolutionary point of view, we could hypothesize that shame has evolved under conditions where survival depended on people abiding by certain norms. They needed to band together to effectively operate as a group and deal better with the terrifying forces of nature. In Palaeolithic times, shame would have been the way to establish a group's pecking order and create the best way of cooperating, shaming people into falling in line. It would be an effective mechanism to establish clear dominance-submission rankings. Interestingly enough, these derivatives of early animalistic behavior patterns can still be observed today, when we tend to take a compliant posture out of shame, or when we subject ourselves to the power and judgment of others.

From a psychological developmental point of view, shame can be seen as a complex emotional response that humans acquire during early child rearing, when children are completely dependent on the bond with their caregivers. It is a very basic emotion – children want to live up to their parent's expectations and when they fail to do so, experience shame. Toddlers exhibit early feelings of embarrassment that can turn into full-blown shame within their first three years of life. Children who are continually criticized, severely punished, neglected, abandoned, or in other ways mistreated quickly get the message that they are inadequate, inferior, or unworthy. These shameful experiences damage the roots from which self-esteem grows. These dysfunctional parenting styles can make children shame-bound.

Hypercritical, perfectionist parents can even make shame a transgenerational pattern by sending the same message they received when they were children to their children – that they are never good enough. Shame raises its head in a very ugly way when children experience traumatic events. It doesn't take much for a child to blame him- or herself when things run out of control. Sexual abuse, in particular, leaves a profound mark. For example, abused children feel shamed by their participation in inappropriate activities. In some instances, children may even internalize and assume the shame that belongs to the adults who emotionally abandon or abuse them. They believe that they are the bad ones. Once children acquire this self-hatred, they are prone to attacks of shame, a pattern that will continue throughout their lives.

Dealing with Shame

Unfortunately, overcoming shame is not easy as it affects the core parts of our personality. The formative wounds of childhood – scars from being teased, bullied, and ostracized by parents, peers, and others – do not heal easily. And to add insult to injury, shame associated with sexual acts complicates the picture. Shame becomes fixed in our core identity – a self that is perceived as fundamentally defective.

Dealing with shame is made even more difficult by our mastery of avoidance and denial. The more powerful the experience of shame, the more we feel compelled to hide those aspects from others, and even from ourselves, preferring to bury it beyond awareness.

But in spite of all these formidable obstacles to healing, people prone to shame should not give up hope. A transformative journey is possible. The first step on this journey of change is realizing that there is no shame in asking for help. The next is to bring the shameful thing to light. After all, a wound that's never exposed will never heal. The ability to discover the origins of shameful experiences is the first stage in taking greater control of our lives and will help us become more attuned to what triggers shame reactions.

Shame-bound people (like Steven) need to learn self-compassion – to embrace who they are and treat themselves with the same respect they show others. They have to learn to recognize when a negative thought spiral begins and to challenge their shame-based thinking. Engaging in these corrective emotional experiences can help them to improve their sense of self-esteem, increase their feelings of worthiness and belonging, foster their self-acceptance, and reduce unhealthy reactions to shame, such as withdrawal and counterattack.

People in the helping professions can play an important role in this healing process. They can help shame-bound individuals realize that they were victims, not the originators, of their trauma. Psychotherapists and coaches can assist shame victims to accept who they really are, put their feelings of shame into perspective, relieve them of their tendency to self-blame, and, eventually, internalize their shadow side. Acquiring this feeling of being good enough, of being worthwhile, of deserving love and acceptance, may be the key to help them transform into their most authentic and, possibly, happier selves.

Steven might have been helped on his journey to recovery by this story. A learned man was once asked to give a speech. His reputation was so high that the hall where he was going to deliver his speech was overflowing with people eager to hear what he had to say. After the master of ceremonies introduced him, the learned man asked the audience,

"Do you know what I am going to say?" "No," came the unanimous answer – upon which the speaker said he had no wish to speak to such ignorant people. With that, he walked out of the auditorium.

But the members of the organizing committee ran after him, begging him to return and give his speech. When he came back, there were even more people in the hall. Again, he asked the audience if they had any idea what he was going to say. This time, the unanimous reply was "Yes!" – upon which the learned man said, "There's no need for me to give a speech, then, as you already know what it's going to be about." And with that, he disappeared once again.

Just as the learned man was getting into his car to drive away, a member of the organizing committee stopped him and persuaded him to return once more. Again, he stood on the stage with the eager crowd in front of him. Again, he asked them if they knew what he was going to say. This time, half the audience said no, while the other half said yes. To which the learned man said, "Great, now the half that knows can tell the half that doesn't what my speech is going to be about." And with that he left for good.

Of course, given Steven's personality makeup, he has some way to go before he has the courage to follow in the learned man's footsteps. But if another opportunity arises for him to give another speech, he could try to make play a part of his interaction with the audience. Too much preparation might have led to rigidity and bored the audience. Steven might have been subconsciously aware that this was happening, contributing to his shame reaction. Playfulness can be a great antidote to stress – and can help reduce shame reactions.

18

What's Pushed Out the Door Will Come Back Through the Window

You have power over your mind—not outside events. Realize this, and you will find strength.
—Marcus Aurelius
Unexpressed emotions will never die. They are buried alive and will come forth later in uglier ways.
—Sigmund Freud

Cyril was the vice president of a large retail operation that had been started by a strong-headed entrepreneur. Unfortunately, the relationship between Cyril and the founder was very turbulent, due to Cyril's allergic reactions to his boss's autocratic leadership style. Cyril found it hard to stand up to bullies – his father had been one. His boss's statement, "I don't have ulcers, I give ulcers," was too close to home. Cyril always made a superhuman effort not to lose his cool with his boss but far too often he would come home fuming after another of their difficult encounters. He would pour himself a drink to relax. The problem was that Cyril was not very good at holding his liquor. Pleasant as he was under normal circumstances, under the influence he turned into a mean-spirited drunk. On a

© The Author(s) 2019
M. F. R. Kets de Vries, *Down the Rabbit Hole of Leadership*,
https://doi.org/10.1007/978-3-319-92462-5_18

number of occasions he had aggressively acted out, assaulting others, and even destroying property. His wife and children remembered vividly one occasion when he had kicked in the door in their house. The next day he acted as if nothing had happened, a typical feature of one of his drinking spells. When confronted with his behavior, his defense would be, "I don't remember." It was as though Cyril preferred to act out rather than work through what troubled him. Instead of saying, "I'm angry with you," he would throw a book at someone, or punch a hole in the wall.

Acting out describes people's impulsive, often negative, and antisocial ways of coping with the anxiety associated with (unconscious) emotional conflicts. These people resort to extreme behavior to express thoughts or feelings they aren't capable of expressing otherwise. Acting out is a defense mechanism whereby repressed or hidden emotions are brought out into the open in destructive ways, like throwing a tantrum, developing an addiction (e.g. drinking, gambling, or compulsive promiscuity) or other-attention seeking activities. Instead of mentally processing undigested, distressing memories, people who act out feel compelled to behave destructively toward themselves and others – without really realizing what they are doing, and why they are doing it.

Putting a lid on troublesome memories or pushing them outdoors is not the answer. Neither is letting sleeping dogs lie: these particular dogs wake easily. When troublesome memories are pushed out of consciousness, they find other ways to come back to haunt us. Interestingly enough, when people who act out are confronted with their destructive behavior, they are reluctant to accept responsibility. One of the reasons for this denial is that the refusal to accept responsibility for their misdeeds mitigates possible feelings of shame and guilt. Given their inability to metabolize undigested issues, however, these people continue to act out even though this behavioral pattern may be destroying their lives. And although acting out might reduce the discomfort they experience in suppressing undigested memories and feelings, it's not the answer to resolving their problems. Acting out doesn't create opportunities to set constructive change in motion.

Acting out is mostly associated with the behavior of children. Temper tantrums are a form of acting out in situations where children do not get their way with a parent. They are a way of expressing distress. Self-harming is also a form of acting out, a way of expressing in physical pain what they are unable to feel emotionally.

Acting out can be a highly effective way of getting parental attention, can become quite prominent in adolescence, manifested through smoking, drinking, drug use, and even shoplifting. All these behavior patterns should be seen as cries for help. However, over time most children learn to substitute these attention-seeking strategies for more socially acceptable and constructive forms of communication. But even in adulthood, some people, like Cyril, continue to act out feelings (rebelliousness, defiance, helplessness, hopelessness) that derive from emotionally charged feelings about people or situations from their childhood.

There is a clear difference between acting out and acting up. Acting-up – consciously and deliberately misbehaving – is not acting out. In most instances, people who behave badly know exactly what they're up to, and why they are doing what they are. They engage in immature, irresponsible behavior of which they're fully aware and which is perfectly within their ability to control. Someone acting inappropriately through acting out is playing out unconscious and unresolved inner issues and are not aware that there are more constructive ways of dealing with them.

How should we treat people who act out as a way of dealing with their intra-psychic, unresolved problems? Is it possible to stop their self-destructive behavior? How can we convince them that they are allowing past memories to affect their current actions? Is it possible to guide these people toward taking responsibility for their actions and have them own their own lives?

By the time they reach adulthood, people who act out should have learned to restrain themselves from demonstrating their emotions in extreme, physical ways. But there will still be times when transference reactions – the redirection of unconscious, emotionally charged emotions and feelings from one person to another – make them regress to childhood behavior patterns. There will be times when all of us will be reminded of our vulnerability and experience unsettling emotions like fear, sadness, helplessness, and humiliation. These disturbing feelings fuel the need to act out.

Much acting out behavior derives from dangers that are long past. People who act out need to acquire the kind of reflective capacity that will enable them to work through these feelings and stop them from acting out in the first place. They need to learn not to act vengefully to people in the present due to unresolved associations with the past. They need to understand the degree to which they are caught up in these transference reactions and realize that the ability to express conflict safely and constructively is an important part of mature development. Constructive ways of dealing with conflict include talking about problems, working with a coach, or psychotherapist, to become more mindfully aware of their underlying issues. The ability to express troublesome feelings is an important part of impulse control, personal development, and self-care.

Cyril clearly experiences the need to rebel against any type of authority figure. Expecting Cyril to follow orders is a recipe for disaster. As he hasn't been able to master legitimate ways of expressing his frustrations, he acts out, and regresses to self-destructive behavior. Cyril has never learned how to work through difficult emotional experiences.

To be able to help a person such as Cyril, it will be important to understand where these reactions come from. Is he dealing with real issues or is he caught up in a transference reaction? Is what's happening to him a distortion of perceptions due to insecurities in his past? Conflict-ridden behavior like Cyril's is driven primarily by unconscious defensiveness rather than normal logic and self-awareness. Obnoxious as his behavior can be, he is a prisoner of his own inner anxieties. If we can accept this, we are more likely to keep our cool when dealing with him, and not take his behavior too personally. People like Cyril act out to protect themselves from uncomfortable thoughts and feelings. If we keep this in mind, we may be able to understand that it's a waste of time to push back against his resistance. Feedback about his dysfunctional behavior may only strengthen his defensiveness. It's not going to be helpful to get into arguments. Defensiveness will only create more defensiveness and interferes with our efforts to get a message across. It will be much more effective to roll with his resistance and use his own momentum to facilitate change.

The best opening position in dealing with people like Cyril is to express empathy. It's important, however, to listen carefully while doing so, and decode what he is saying. Whatever information we gain from this interchange should be reflected back to him. This is a great way to build rapport. It will also be helpful to explore the discrepancy between his present behavior and what he wishes for the future. This kind of mutual exploration will be more likely to motivate him to embark on change. Subsequently, we might encourage him to find solutions to his own problems – to make him responsible for whatever change is needed. In my experience, while people like Cyril might initially resist, they will usually be the first to highlight the problems they are facing. While Cyril is engaged in trying to solve his problems, he can also be recruited to help develop solutions. Over time he will come to understand that acting out has consequences for which he is responsible. He will learn that things are not happening to him; they are happening because of him.

Here's a symbolic tale about looking for reasons in the right place. Walking down the street, a woman sees someone on his hands and knees, obviously looking for something. She stops and asks him what he is doing. He answers that he's looking for a ring he's dropped, so the woman joins him in the search. After a while they have still had no luck, so she asks the man where exactly he had been standing when he dropped the ring. To her surprise, the man points to a spot several meters away. The woman says, "But if you lost the ring in the doorway, why are we looking for it out here?" And the man says, "Because here there's more light."

19

What Good Is Empathy?

We think we listen, but very rarely do we listen with real understanding, true empathy. Yet listening, of this very special kind, is one of the most potent forces for change that I know.
—Carl Rogers
Human morality is unthinkable without empathy.
—Frans de Waal

The telecommunications company's offsite strategy meeting was running smoothly. For days, its executives had been preparing intensively for the final presentations. Their challenge was how to find ways their company could engage in a major transformation process. Having done their preliminary work, all of them were curious about how their suggestions for strategic renewal would be received by the CEO and the executive team. Would their reactions be positive?

A relative newcomer was volunteered to make the opening presentation. In the middle of her lively introduction, the CEO's mobile phone rang. To everybody's surprise, the CEO took the call, walked out of the room, and reappeared 30 minutes later. In his absence, the presenter tried

© The Author(s) 2019
M. F. R. Kets de Vries, *Down the Rabbit Hole of Leadership*,
https://doi.org/10.1007/978-3-319-92462-5_19

to continue, but was clearly unsure how to proceed while her boss was absent. After the CEO's return, the steam seemed to have gone out of the presenter. The discussion that followed floundered. To many, it was an opportunity lost.

Incidents like this had occurred before. Many felt that their CEO was insensitive to other people's needs. But his lack of empathy with his subordinates would cost him dearly. As the strategy meeting was a washout, the expected corporate transformation process never took off. Soon after, the company's lack of strategic agility contributed to a steep loss in market share, a declining stock price, and a revolt by its major shareholders, which ended in the dismissal of the CEO. Subsequently, most of the members of the executive team were replaced while hundreds of employees were dismissed. Clearly, not paying attention to the thoughts and intentions of others could make the difference between corporate success and failure.

But what is empathy? It's derived from the Greek words "*em*" and "*pathos*," literally meaning "into feeling." Empathy refers to our ability to resonate with the feelings of others – to imaginatively share the emotional experience of another person. An ingenious way to sum up empathy is "your pain in my heart." When we are empathic, we are fully present to what's alive in the other person in the moment; we comprehend why another person is doing what he or she is doing. To use some everyday expression, we are able to see things through someone else's eyes. Empathy also relates to our ability to make sense of what is or isn't being said or what is or isn't being done. When we are empathetic, we enhance our ability to receive and process information. It is a key ingredient of successful relationships as it helps us understand the perspectives, needs, and intentions of others. Empathy, however, will always involve some kind of guesswork. We'll never completely know how the other person feels. However, we can try to imagine their feelings, given what we have learned about them.

Empathy is a key dimension of emotional intelligence, that is, the ability to recognize our emotions, understand what they're telling us, and to realize how they affect people around us. It's a core component in every human relationship – a cornerstone of interpersonal effectiveness. Empathy helps us understand the unspoken elements of our communication with others. It enables us to be more effective at collaboration and finding solutions.

The term empathy is often used interchangeably with sympathy or compassion but it is not the same thing. Sympathy refers to feelings of compassion, sorrow, or pity for the hardships another person encounters, while being empathic implies putting ourselves in the shoes of others and understanding what they are feeling. When we express sympathy, we acknowledge another person's emotional hardships; we have compassion for them, but we don't necessarily feel what they are feeling. With sympathy we feel for others; with empathy, we feel with them.

Human morality is unthinkable without empathy. But how can we develop it? How does it come about? Most of our ability to correctly read and respond to another's emotions derives from childhood – what we learned from our parents, and other caregivers. Most likely, empathy started out as an evolutionary developmental mechanism to improve maternal care. Mothers who were attentive to their offspring's needs would be much more likely to rear successful offspring.

There may also be a neurological component to empathy. The chemical currency of empathy is controlled by a group of neurotransmitters that make us feel good, endorphins, dopamine, serotonin, and oxytocin. Oxytocin in particular seems to play an important role as it is released when people bond socially. Oxytocin helps us to be more aware of the pain of others.

Being empathic has also many benefits from a business perspective. It can be viewed as a soft tool in an executive toolkit that contributes to hard, tangible results. In general, people who are empathic are better leaders and followers. The deceptively simple practice of caring about the well-being of others creates a sense of reciprocity in relationships. What's more, empathy begets empathy.

Empathic executives are more attuned to the needs of people around them. They are better at managing relationships and relating to others. They are more likely to establish trust, creating safer environments to work in. Empathy also facilitates collaboration. No wonder empathic people are better at teamwork. Working in an empathic organization has a stress-reducing effect. It makes for a more committed workforce and greater motivation to achieve company goals.

But in spite of these benefits, many (often successful) executives are direly lacking in empathy. There are myriad reasons why this is so. Much has to do with their specific character makeup. Self-centered and narcissistic people, described in earlier chapters, find it difficult to put themselves in other people's shoes. Others may even possess sociopathic traits – these people see others as commodities; they project an air of sincerity but in reality their behavior is all window-dressing. Any form of self-absorption kills empathy, so these types of people find it hard to sustain close committed relationships and friendships. In our increasingly network-oriented society the lack of empathy comes with a steep price attached.

To acquire empathy, we have to learn how to see ourselves from the outside and others from the inside and the first step to doing this is to understand ourselves. We need to recognize and accept our own feelings. To start with, we have to learn how to be good listeners (including listening to ourselves). Although this sounds deceptively easy, it's not. In our digital age, when we are ready prey to many distractions, it's difficult not to be a multi-tasker. To be truly empathic, we need to be fully present when dealing with others. This means that in the company of others we don't check our emails, don't look at our watch, and don't take calls. We need to be mindfully aware of our surroundings, especially the behaviors and expressions of other people. To acquire this kind of sensitivity, we need to show a genuine interest in the other.

Remaining non-judgmental is another challenge in developing empathy. It's not easy to figure out how our feelings affect our perceptions, but too easy to pass judgment about whether the other person is right or wrong. We must take care not to dismiss other people's concerns out of hand, not to interrupt when they are talking, not to rush into giving our opinion. To quote Molière, "One should examine oneself for a very long time before thinking of condemning others."

Challenging our own preconceived notions implies listening actively to what the other person has to say to make sure that we understand it. This means also tuning in to non-verbal communication. People often communicate what they think or feel non-verbally, even when their verbal communication says something quite different.

Is empathy declining in our narcissistic age? Are we living with an empathy deficit? It's difficult to tell, although in our increasingly interconnected world, cooperation and communication are more important than ever before. Much of our world's insensibility and hardness is due to a lack of imagination that prevents awareness of others' experiences. If everyone had the ability to truly empathize, the world would be a much better place.

Of course, empathy can be taken *ad absurdum*, as this short tale shows. A wise man was asked to be the arbiter in a complicated case. One of the two parties delivered a long soliloquy about the bad behavior of the other. After listening and reflecting carefully, the wise man said, "You're right." Then it was the turn of the second man to speak. He also gave a very impassioned speech about how wrong the first man was. After some thought, the wise man said, "You're right."

At this point, one of the witnesses stood up and said, "Hang on, how can two people with such very different opinions both be right?" To which the wise man replied, "You're right."

Now everyone was exasperated. Then both men stood, and said to the wise man, "You're right. We'll settle the matter between the two of us."

20

Are You Suffering from D.A.D.?

We cannot, in a moment, get rid of habits of a lifetime.
—Mahatma Gandhi
Every form of addiction is bad, no matter whether the narcotic be alcohol or morphine or idealism.
—Carl Jung

I'm not questioning your relationship with your father. I'm talking about digital addiction disorder. Recently, I ran a workshop and one of the participants (I'll call her Anne) had to excuse herself regularly to leave the room. I assumed she had a weak bladder or an upset stomach but I later found out that she was suffering from D.A.D. In layman's terms, D.A.D. is the inability to stop looking at your computer, mobile phone, or tablet. This particular workshop is reflective and participants are not supposed to use electronic equipment, but Anne was physically unable to wait for the breakout period. She felt compelled to check and respond to whatever messages were coming in.

When I talked to her, I learned that Anne spent an extraordinary amount of time on social networking, online gaming, and online bidding

© The Author(s) 2019
M. F. R. Kets de Vries, *Down the Rabbit Hole of Leadership*,
https://doi.org/10.1007/978-3-319-92462-5_20

sites. She was also addicted to watching YouTube video clips. When I asked Anne why she spent so much time on the Internet, this highly stressed person replied in all seriousness that "being connected" relaxed her. That's when I realized she was suffering from D.A.D. Her excessive use of electronic media had become uncontrollable and interfered seriously with her daily life. Symptomatically, D.A.D. resembles impulse-control and obsessive-compulsive disorders.

The latest edition of the psychiatrists' bible, *The Diagnostic and Statistical Manual of Mental Disorders*, does not (yet) include D.A.D. as a mental health disorder. Though prevalent in society, and emerging as a problematic phenomenon, D.A.D. still needs a considerable amount of research. Studies are even uncertain whether D.A.D. is a disorder in its own right or a symptom of other underlying conditions. But whatever we call it, D.A.D. presents a compulsive behavior pattern that completely takes over the addict's life.

As D.A.D. is becoming a significant health threat, the time has come to recognize this disorder as a separate and distinct behavioral addiction. For example, surveys in the United States and Europe have indicated alarming prevalence rates that range between 1.5% and 8.2% of the general population. The estimates are even higher in the Far East, where 30% or more of the population are experiencing problematic Internet use.[1] (The widely variable differences in percentages can be explained by the fact that so far there are no standardized criteria for measuring this addiction.) As a caveat, I should say that using the Internet intensively doesn't mean you are an addict or that you suffer from D.A.D. It only becomes a real disorder when it begins to seriously interfere with healthy functioning in your daily life. It seems that people can become addicted to escaping reality in much the same way as they become addicted to alcohol and drugs.

Healthy functioning is based on the premise of balance. In its obsessiveness, digital addiction is comparable to addictions to food, alcohol, or other drugs. All addictions influence the brain – both in the connections between brain cells, and in the areas of the brain that control attention, executive functions and emotional processing. The release of dopamine,

---

[1] http://online.liebertpub.com/doi/abs/10.1089/cyber.2014.0317?journalCode=cyber

triggered by the addictive substance, provides a temporary high on which addicts become dependent. One reason why this happens might be that the addict's levels of dopamine and serotonin are deficient compared to the general population. We can hypothesize that people with a digital addiction have fewer dopamine receptors in certain areas of the brain or other kinds of impairment of dopamine functioning. Consequently, they have difficulties experiencing normal levels of pleasure in activities that most people find rewarding. To increase pleasure, these D.A.D.-prone individuals seek greater than average engagement in digital activities that stimulate an increase in dopamine release, effectively giving them more rewards but also creating a state of dependency.

What kinds of people are more likely to become addicts? And what are the symptoms of D.A.D.?

Being stressed out – suffering from anxiety and depression – can be a contributing factor in the development of addictions. People who suffer from D.A.D. may be vulnerable to other addictions, such as alcohol, drugs, sex, or gambling. People who have relationship issues also seem to be at greater risk of developing an Internet addiction. They use digital connections to boost their spirits and escape from their problems. The time devoted to cyber-relationships comes at the expense of time spent with the real people in their lives. Connecting with a virtual fantasy world replaces the complexities and richness of real-life human connections. Some addicts may even construct a secret life, creating alternative online personas in an attempt to mask unsavory online behavior. Many of these addicts (Anne is a good example) become restless, moody, anxious, depressed, or irritable if blocked from their digital activities. Other D.A.D.s may suffer from physical symptoms like digestive problems, headaches, eating disorders, obesity, backaches, poor personal hygiene, carpal tunnel syndrome, neck pain, sleep disturbance, dry eyes, and other visual problems. Interestingly, when asked about their Internet involvement, D.A.D.s conceal the extent of their participation. But in their need to connect to strangers, they can neglect family obligations, destroy their social life, and lose out on significant job, educational, and career opportunities.

Unfortunately, the cure for D.A.D., like most addictions, is an uphill struggle. Treatment will not be straightforward, since most of us have to use the Internet to some degree (or even a lot) on a daily basis. In that way, D.A.D. is comparable to food addictions, where it's impossible to go cold turkey. The process involved learning healthy eating patterns and creating a better balance. Also, unlike recovering alcoholics who must abstain from drinking for life, in today's world total digital abstinence is not a feasible option. Digital detox is a formidable challenge.

Some professionals have suggested that medications can be effective in the treatment of D.A.D. They argue that if you are prone to this condition, it's likely that you also suffer from anxiety and depression. From a psychopharmacological perspective, the use of anti-anxiety medication or anti-depressants is a promising avenue of treatment. From a psychological point of view, cognitive-behavioral therapy is frequently the treatment of choice. D.A.D. addicts can learn to replace damaging thought and behavior patterns with healthier, more productive ones. Mindfulness-based stress reduction training and group psychotherapy have also proved helpful. Support groups (compensating for a lack of social support), and various forms of family therapy that address relational family problems can be quite successful. Other professionals suggest a multi-modal treatment approach, implementing several different types of treatment (pharmacology, individual and group psychotherapy, and family counseling) simultaneously.

Sadly, their preoccupation with the Internet has become the organizing principle of some people's lives. It is important, however, to recognize that D.A.D. is a warning sign: it indicates a special kind of pain that begs for understanding. We can only help digital addicts by understanding the nature of their pain. Going offline is the test of sanity. Disconnection may be the real way to connect.

Here's a coaching story about digital addiction. An executive visited his coach and told her, "My life is miserable. Not only have I got to deal with my wife, my three children, and my mother-in-law but there is the Internet. Each day I get hundreds of emails and notifications from Facebook and LinkedIn. I'm going crazy." The coach asked if he was on WhatsApp? "Not yet," he said. "Why don't you add that to your repertoire?" said the coach. The executive was taken aback by her unexpected reaction but as he was completely desperate he followed her advice. A week later, he was back to see his coach again. "Life's no better," he said "In fact, it's much worse with WhatsApp. People are flooding me with pointless messages." "Oh dear," said the coach. "Why don't you add Twitter? That might help." But that did no good, either, as the executive made quite clear to his coach when he berated her a week later. "Get Instagram," she advised. The following week, the executive showed up more miserable than ever. Shouting at his coach, he said he was drowning in emails, blogs, tweets, video clips, photos, and other messages. He had no time for his family, he had no time to see his friends, he wasn't getting nearly enough sleep, and he was close to a nervous breakdown. The coach said, "Why don't you delete everything and see what happens?" The executive followed her advice, and returned a few days later, saying, "My life is wonderful. I've never had so much peace."

21

Accepting Your Shadow Side

There is but one cause of human failure. And that is man's lack of faith in his true Self.
—William James

Everyone carries a shadow, and the less it is embodied in the individual's conscious life, the blacker and denser it is. At all counts, it forms an unconscious snag, thwarting our most well-meant intentions.
—Carl Jung

During one of my workshops on the psychodynamics of leadership I met a senior banker named Tina. Our conversations revealed someone at a crossroads in life, although Tina wasn't conscious that she had several possible paths to choose from. She had little interest in her work. It had become routine – a drain on her energy. She couldn't remember the last time she had been happy. For some time, she had been asking herself whether she should quit. But quitting was easier said than done. What would her colleagues and bosses think of her? After all, she had been very successful in running the firm's principal trading desk. And what about her personal finances? Could she afford to quit?

© The Author(s) 2019
M. F. R. Kets de Vries, *Down the Rabbit Hole of Leadership*,
https://doi.org/10.1007/978-3-319-92462-5_21

Our conversation started a process of reflection that initially raised more questions. But these questions were deeper and more revealing. What if what she had been doing was in response to what others expected her to do? Banking had been a tradition in her family. Her father had been a banker, and so had her grandfather.

Tina had been her parents' golden girl, excellent at school, a star student at an Ivy League college, and had an MBA from one of the world's premier business schools. She married a man her parents approved of, and settled into a traditional banker's life. Now, at the age of 45, she was wondering whether all her efforts had been worth it. Were the choices she had made actually pseudo-choices, given her family's expectations of her? And even more frightening: what other choices did she have at this point in her life?

Tina also wondered whether her confused state of mind had something to do with the fact that her youngest child had just left for college and that the house had abruptly become very quiet. It didn't help that her husband was preoccupied with his own pursuits.

And then there were her disturbing dreams. She kept dreaming about being lost in strange places. A major theme of another uncanny dream was not getting what she wanted. These dreams left Tina feeling anxious and frustrated. In some of the dreams, she hardly recognized herself. In those dreams she did exactly what she wanted, and did it forcefully. Some of her dreams featured disturbing sexual imagery.

These dreams seemed to be messages from a hidden part of herself – aspects of her personality that she found difficult to reconcile. Was it possible that her dreams were trying to tell her something that she didn't want to hear in daily life? One thing was clear: these dreams, combined with her deep questions about her life choices and experiences, made her question whether she was doing what she really wanted to do. Had the way she lived her life so far made a difference? What was it all worth, in the end?

Tina increasingly began to question her identity as a career woman, wife, and mother. Would she be able to give up being perfect for everyone else, and just be herself? She remembered how as an adolescent she had been preoccupied with wondering what people wanted her to do or to be.

Perhaps, the time had come to revisit these questions and take an honest look at what *she* wanted to do, not what others expected her to do.

Tina's self-questioning not only made her confused, it also overwhelmed her with a deep sense of regret at not having made her own choices. Bewildered as she was, she was now questioning everything about her life. Was she having a delayed identity crisis?

A number of well-known psychologists have talked about identity. For example, Carl Jung introduced the notion of the shadow side of our personality. He viewed "the shadow" as our unknown, dark side – dark both because it is predominantly made up of the primitive, negative, socially or religiously depreciated human emotions such as sexuality, striving for power, selfishness, greed, envy, jealousy, and anger, but dark also because it personifies everything we fear and refuse to acknowledge. Unless we come to terms with our shadow side, we are condemned to become its unwitting victim. In some ways, Tina's shadow can be seen as her unlived life – unlived because of her compliance with her parents' and others' expectations and wishes. But at this stage in her life, can she still learn to accept or even enhance this part of herself?

The psychoanalyst Erik Erikson introduced the idea of identity crisis. According to Erikson, establishing a sense of identity is one of the most important challenges that we face during our life's journey. In his developmental scheme, puberty (one of the core reference points in the human life cycle) is associated with heightened susceptibility to developmental changes. The various bodily transformations that happen during that period, i.e. sexual and muscular development, and changes in cognitive structure, evolve what once was our childhood self. Puberty is a period of great turmoil and confusion. Stabilization of our identity occurs only when we (as adolescents) have explored and committed ourselves to the salient aspects of what our life's purpose is going to be. Also, Erikson suggests that identity formation has a dark and negative side. There are parts of us that are attractive but disturbing and therefore tend to be submerged. In the process of becoming an adult, we not only internalize what's viewed as acceptable, we also internalize (if only subliminally) our parents' (and society's) attitudes toward undesirable qualities and characteristics. But these undesirables turn into forbidden fruit. To feel more authentic, however, we may have to integrate these forbidden fruits into our personality structure.

Another well-known psychoanalyst and pediatrician, Donald Winnicott, elaborated on the idea of the "true" and "false" self. Winnicott explained that beginning in infancy, all of us, in response to perceived threats to our well-being, develop a defensive structure that may evolve into a false self. He suggests that if our basic needs are not acknowledged – not mirrored back to us by our parents – we might presume they are unimportant. Complying with our parents' desires, we may repress our own desires, not actualizing what we would really like to do. We may believe that non-compliance endangers our role in the family. In addition, we may internalize our parents' dreams of self-glorification through our achievements. Sometimes, we may even be sent on mission impossible, accomplishing what they were unable to do. But this acquiescence to the wishes of others is an emotional lie. It comes at the price of suppressing our own needs. In our efforts to please others, we hide and deny our true self, which in turn leads to self-estrangement. If that's the case, the false self will get the upper hand. It becomes a defensive armor to keep the true self at bay and hidden.

If there is too great a discrepancy between the true and the false self, it will create a vulnerable sense of identity. And if we are unable to acquire a stable sense of identity we may end up unraveling one day, as Tina did. Tina was experiencing what Erikson would call a delayed identity crisis. At a certain point in her life, it became difficult for her keep up the lie.

Tina's case demonstrates that the journey of identity exploration at adolescence doesn't stop there. In her case, confronted with new challenges and experiences, the tension between her false and true self came to a head, renewing the confusion she had experienced at an earlier stage of life. Not living a full, complete life – not integrating other parts of herself, her shadow or negative identity – turned out to be extremely draining, contributing to life choices that didn't answer her real needs.

But the "return of the repressed," as Freud described experiences like Tina's, should not be seen as purely negative. Although Tina might have seen these aspects of herself as representing an unlived life, her delayed identity crisis also contained the seeds of psychological renewal – the motivation to take new directions in life. Romancing her shadow – accepting the unlived parts of herself and learning to read the messages contained in her shadow side – led her to a deeper level of consciousness, and sparked her imagination. Her buried desires raised the question "Who am I?" and "Who do I want to be?"

In Tina's case, the workshop on the psychodynamics of leadership created a tipping point for change. What could have led to a negative spiral of self-pity turned into the opposite. She came to grips with her earlier life experiences. Her self-exploration gave her greater awareness both of her inner theater and her life journey up to this moment. She realized that this process had private as well as more public phases. She captured her dreams in a journal, and wrote about the associations that came to her. She wrote letters to her past and future self. She told her husband about her dreams and the emotions they evoked. Together they talked about her feelings of frustration and anxiety. Her husband began sharing some of his dreams with her, as well. Their conversations eventually took a more concrete turn, as they discussed their future together, including their finances. Reassured and invigorated, Tina took a hard look at her work responsibilities and saw ways that she could make changes that would benefit the bank as well as herself. She even got into an argument about politics with her father at the dinner table, and to her great surprise, he seemed to respect her opinion.

Tina had sorted out some of the demons in her inner experiences. The moments of free association and reflection had led to meaningful conversations with important people in her life. She felt she had liberated herself from the shackles that were holding her back from realizing her full potential. She accepted what she learned about herself without judgment. In the process, she came to terms with her shadow side, creating the rapprochement needed between her false and true self. She realized she had only just begun a fascinating adventure, and she was curious to continue her exploration of the riches contained in this previously unknown world inside herself.

I will end with a Zen story about the need to get to grips with your shadow side. Two monks, one old, one young, were traveling together to a distant monastery. After a long journey, they arrived at a fast-flowing river. On the bank, they met a very beautiful young woman who was in tears. When they asked her what was the matter, she said she had to see her mother who lived on the other side, but that she was afraid the current was too strong for her to cross. Without hesitation, the older monk picked up the woman and carried her across the river. The two monks left her on the opposite bank and continued their journey. For a while, the younger monk was very silent. Then, no longer able to control himself, he blurted out, "As monks, aren't we forbidden to deal with women? How could you carry that woman on your back?" To which the older monk replied, "I just carried her to the other side of the river, but it seems that you are still carrying her."

22

Beyond Coaching BS

It is not only what we do but also what we do not for which we are accountable.
—Molière
The mind is not a vessel to be filled, but a fire to be kindled.
—Plutarch

I find myself increasingly intimidated by people in the executive coaching world. Reading their resumés gives me a sense of unease about my own abilities. According to their narratives, these coaches have so much to offer. How can I reach the Olympian heights they profess to have reached? Will I ever be able to (and I quote) "unlock my clients' dormant potential... provide them with a sense of self-fulfillment; and have them acquire a growth mindset?" Can I too "deepen my clients' learning, improve their performance, and enhance their quality of life, both personally and/or professionally?" Do I have the deep knowledge to ask them really challenging questions? And will I be patient enough to let them come up with the answers?

© The Author(s) 2019
M. F. R. Kets de Vries, *Down the Rabbit Hole of Leadership*,
https://doi.org/10.1007/978-3-319-92462-5_22

Apparently, many of these executive coaches who broadcast their expertise are convinced that they can do all these things. To support their claims, they get their clients to testify how great they are. According to their clients' accounts, without their coach they would never have been as successful as they are now. Their coaches have helped them to reach their maximum potential; their coaches' life-changing interventions turned them into exceptional leaders.

The Lofty Promises of Executive Coaching

Amidst the boom of executive coaches, an even more elevated type of coach exists: the Master Coach. Master Coaches differentiate themselves from the pack; they are "always on the lookout for the things [their clients] don't want to see, and listen for the things they don't want to hear." They are their clients' early warning system. They help them self-actualize and bring their clients to places they never thought they would ever be able to reach.

These self-descriptions of exceptionally qualified Master Coaches have an even more negative effect on my self-confidence. I start to ask myself whether I have what it takes? Could I ever rise to the heights of one of these "masters"? What do I need to do to join their ranks?

According to the websites of some of these Master Coaches, an important part of achieving this elevated status seems to be an accounting game, requiring a minimum of 2500–10,000 hours (14 solid months) of direct coaching experience. Really? Master Training Programs, offering various forms of supervision and other services, can help you reach that target. These figures make me very dubious about the relative importance these programs give to quality and quantity. In the numbers game, there is a propensity toward garbage in, garbage out.

Another requirement for becoming a Master Coach is to regularly practice "self-coaching." According to some of these masters, self-coaching contributes to an "integrity cleanse" that will "allow your soul to emerge and to be seen." Now, what does this mean? Am I just bumbling about in my occasional forays into executive coaching?

Of course, the advantage of being a Master Coach is that you will get "extraordinary coaching results; have more fun; and be more fulfilled." You will also make more money, a none-too-subtle reminder of the financial benefits of being one of this rare breed.

If being a Master Coach is not stratospheric enough, an even more select group is the Most Trusted Advisor. According to the literature on this subject, these unusually talented people are exceptional in understanding their clients' "underlying needs, not just their wants." Compared to mere run-of-the-mill executive coaches, Most Trusted Advisors "provide depth and breadth of knowledge, have unusual listening skills, ask great questions, provide deep insights, and know how to synthesize whatever information they come across." Furthermore, they are "reliable, credible, personable, passionate, authentic, and know how to connect emotionally." They also provide their clients with an "Echo," "Anchor," "Mirror," and "Spark" function. Having earned their clients' "unwavering trust," they are honest brokers, putting their clients' interests before their own.

I must confess that I don't understand the subtle differences in the skills that apparently set an executive coach, a Master Coach, and a Most Trusted Advisor apart. These purportedly unique skills still seem to boil down to the basic functions of a coach – to give clients honest support and help them clarify where they should be going. But perhaps knowing how to "Spark" their clients' vision gives them an edge. People seem to think so, as these coaches apparently build lasting relationships with their clients. In short, they are the supermen and superwomen of the coaching world.

Obviously executive coaches, Master Coaches, and Most Trusted Advisors have designed sophisticated coaching frameworks to help them fight the good fight. They rely heavily on acronyms and at times, I do wonder why.

For example, some of these Master Coaches use the **FUEL** model in their transformative work: this means they **F**rame the conversation, **U**nderstand the current state, **E**xplore the desired state, and **L**ay out a success plan. Even better, they might draw on the **GROW** model: **G**oal, Current **R**eality, **O**ptions, and **W**ill or **W**ay forward. Then there is the **Three Ps** model: **P**erspectives – how they can bring the two worlds of coach and client together; **P**urpose – what is ultimately wanted from the coaching experience; and **P**rocess – how coach and client should work together to achieve the outcome. And if that's not enough there is the rather less literate **STEPPPA** model: where **S** stands for **S**ubject, **T** for **T**arget, **E** for **E**motion, **P** for **P**erception, **P**lan, and **P**ace, and **A** for **A**ct. And this is just a sample. There are many other transformative coaching acronyms out there.

Beyond the Coaching BS

These categories of coaches and coaching models make me uncomfortable. They strike me as a marketing segmentation plot to fool the gullible. Many of these descriptions are just psychobabble that relies heavily on psychological jargon and expressions. The people who resort to this kind of language often have little or no real training in psychology. In my lengthy experience, as a psychoanalyst and clinical professor of leadership, the psychological dynamics that guide human behavior are far from neat. Human behavior doesn't fit into boxes or categories. While these acronyms facilitate simple visual and verbal recognition, they confuse the nuances of human dynamics; they are simply fads. The oversimplified models they represent fail to build an understanding of what's really happening in the coach-client interface.

I also believe that the coaching profession is doing itself no favors by exaggerating what it has to offer. Contrary to all the hype found in the literature of coaching training programs, creating behavior change isn't easy, or fast, or linear. There are no miraculous cures. As any psychiatrist, psychoanalyst or clinical psychologist will tell you, behavior change is hard work. There will be many setbacks when embarking on this kind of endeavor. In most interventions it's always two steps forward, one step back. The exaggerated promises made by executive coaches, Master Coaches, and Most Trusted Advisors create highly unrealistic expectations.

The promises made by many of these coaches and coaching programs amount to little more than a questionable sales pitch. And I strongly believe that the lack of truth in their advertising debases the currently unregulated coaching profession. It's high time to debunk the jargon and shallowness behind the current proliferation of what's called executive coaching. In its place, we need richer frameworks to define the kind of work coaches are capable of, as well as ways of assessing the quality of their coaching interventions.

The American jurist Oliver Wendell Holmes Jr. once said: "A mind that is stretched by a new experience can never go back to its old dimensions." Coaching as the language of change and learning has a salient role to play. It's important, however, to stay grounded and not turn coaching into yet into another executive fad.

The hype created by these so-called Master Coaches reminds me of Molière's play *Le Bourgeois gentilhomme*, a satire describing the pretentiousness of Monsieur Jourdain, the son of a cloth merchant who goes to great lengths to rise above his middle-class background. He wants to be viewed as an aristocrat and makes a fool of himself as he tries to learn the sort of activities suitable for a gentleman.

To help him he hires a number of people who take advantage of him: sneering music, dance, and philosophy teachers and an impoverished aristocrat who exploits his pretensions. In a famous scene, Monsieur Jourdain's philosophy teacher tells him that he has been "speaking prose" his entire life, which Monsieur Jourdain takes as the revelation of an innate aristocratic skill:

Monsieur Jourdain:	So when I say, "Nicole, bring me my slippers and fetch my nightcap," is that prose?
Philosophy master:	Indubitably.
Monsieur Jourdain:	Well, what do you know? These past 40 years, I've been speaking in prose without knowing it! I'm so grateful to you for teaching me that!

And what brings this famous scene from Molière's play so forcefully to my mind is my fervent wish that these Master Coaches and Most Trusted Advisors would also speak prose, instead of psychobabble, and stop exploiting their clients.

23

What Happened to Prince and Princess Charming?

The great question that has never been answered, and which I have not yet been able to answer, despite my thirty years of research into the feminine soul, is "What does a woman want?"
—Sigmund Freud
The meeting of two personalities is like the contact of two chemical substances: if there is any reaction, both are transformed.
—Carl Jung

Let's admit it, deep down we are all suckers for fairy tales. We like the kinds of stories where princes or princesses get their beloved. Stories like *Cinderella* or *Sleeping Beauty* are very much part of our collective unconscious. The fact that millions of people all over the world were glued to their television sets observing the fairy tale-like marriage of Prince Harry and Meghan Markle demonstrates the timelessness of these kinds of stories. After all, a mixed-race American feminist divorcée and soap actress marrying into the world's most traditional royal family is hardly an everyday event. And it is hard to deny that the pomp and circumstance around the marriage satisfied our wildest expectations. But as in all fairy tales, our

© The Author(s) 2019
M. F. R. Kets de Vries, *Down the Rabbit Hole of Leadership*,
https://doi.org/10.1007/978-3-319-92462-5_23

next entreaty is to have them live happily ever after. But how likely is this to happen? The absence of every member of the bride's family except her mother was dwelt on with relish by both the mainstream and social media. The cynical and exploitative attention paid to the bride's father, and the general labeling of both families as "dysfunctional," raises some questions about their likelihood of living happily ever after.

Whatever the reasons for the absence of the bride's family, this glorious wedding illustrates once more the enigma of partner choice. What really makes a relationship click? What kind of chemistry is needed to bring two apparently very different people together and make it work? Partnership often appears to be an obscure and whimsical process that transcends rationality, evolutionary laws, cultural pressures, or even our conscious intentions. What motivates us to select one person over another? Was George Bernard Shaw right when he noted, "Love is a gross exaggeration of the difference between one person and everybody else?"

When it comes to making choices, we could make a distinction between the approach of maximizers (who are looking for Mr. or Ms. Perfect) and satisficers (looking for Mr. or Ms. Good Enough). But as many people have learned the hard way, the notion of the ideal spouse is illusory: reality rarely lives up to what's desired. What muddles the situation even more is that the players in this drama may not be very clear about what kind of attributes are needed to make a relationship a success. The mismatch between ideal and actual partner is a costly and stressful proposition for both the individual and society. If the frequency of divorce is a signifier, far too many people choose the wrong partner. And among those who do not divorce, too many stay in relationships that make them unhappy. Not many people spent time reflecting on the qualities they look for in a partner. And some, following the dictum of hope over experience, repeat the same mistakes over and over again.

Partner choice is an issue that resurfaces over and over again in the executive programs I lead. As I take a holistic orientation to management and career issues (showing the interconnectedness of private and public life, particularly as the participants enter my programs at midlife) messy partner relationships regularly become a topic of discussion.

When participants refer to their partners, a lengthy list of complaints is rolled out. Some of the more typical include being unappreciated, being subjected to too much control, lack of intimacy, flirtatious behavior by one of the partners, a lack of fair process in running the household, and upsetting and disrespectful untidiness.

When I ask my participants why they got into these relationships in the first place, they typically stall, unable to come up with answers immediately. Eventually, some of the more predictable responses are the fear of ending up alone (societal pressures having forced them into making a hasty decision), a ticking biological clock (for women) or low self-esteem, not daring to pursue for the most suitable partner (this creates a warped selection process from day one, and makes failure a self-fulfilling prophecy). On further exploration, some even realize that their selection of a partner was driven by feelings of incompleteness. They made the choice with the not necessarily conscious expectation that their partner would complete them. Others seem to complicate matters even further by seeing their partner as a project, hoping to "fix" or "save" them.

From an evolutionary perspective, the urge for procreation drives partner choice, as men look for the most fertile women, and women look for protectors and good providers who can take care of them and their children. Of course, this proposition is over-simplistic. Many other variables, apart from procreation, come into the partner choice equation. And these variables may change over time: what we look for in a partner when we are in our twenties may be quite different when we are in our thirties, forties, or fifties.

Predictably, when I push the participants in my programs to reflect on their selection criteria, they mention physical attractiveness. But after some consideration, many other variables come to the fore, such as earnings potential, ambition, kindness, and intelligence, even though men and women weigh these factors differently. It has to be acknowledged, however, that there is a substantial sensual dimension to the selection process. It also becomes clear that apart from physical attraction, many people end up in partnerships due to similarity and proximity. Being in the right place at the right time plays a significant role. Exposure to and familiarity with the people we spend time with has a strong bonding effect.

Attachment Behavior

However, to make sense of any form of partner choice, we need to have a basic understanding of the psychodynamics of attachment behavior. John Bowlby, known for his pioneering work on this subject, referred to the idea of the secure base. For example, he noted, "All of us, from cradle to grave, are happiest when life is organized as a series of excursions, long or short, from the secure base provided by our attachment figures".[1] Research shows that we can distinguish three types of attachment patterns: secure, anxious, or avoidant, with secure attachment being the most adaptive of the three. And although in our search for partners, similarity or complementarity may serve as cognitive and emotional criteria in the selection process, the underlying driving force seems to be a search for attachment security – the kind of landing that creates a secure base.

While growing up, a great deal of unconscious imprinting takes place. And as a number of studies have shown, especially with respect to facial and bodily features, girlfriends match mothers and boyfriends match fathers.[2] Furthermore, emotional closeness to a parent seems to increase the likelihood that our partner will resemble that parent. Most likely, we are unconsciously attracted to partners who resemble our parents in one way or another. In addition, to complicate matters, we may also engage in a parallel process, searching in the other for what was missing from our parents and the way we would have liked them to have treated us.

Without realizing it, we may use our partner as the arena in which to deal with the unfinished business of childhood. Although consciously we may assure ourselves we will not repeat the mistakes our parents made, there is always the danger of unconscious sabotage, given the deep desire to repair what went wrong in the parent-child relationship. Trying to right the wrongs of childhood all too often leads paradoxically to the repetition of the same behavior patterns as our parents. These unconscious dynamics may explain the attraction for Mr. or Ms. Wrong. This dysfunctional selection process is fueled by the fact that choosing Mr. or Ms. Wrong can be very exciting: we know it's the wrong choice, but we

---

[1] Bowlby (1988).

[2] https://link.springer.com/article/10.1007/s12144-000-1015-7

get a neurotic kick out of it. Some bad choices can also be interpreted as ways to avoid commitment due to fears of intimacy. To compound the drama, there may be some pleasure attached to making neurotic choices. This kind of secondary gain may prompt people to play the role of martyr to invite sympathy.

The Rules of the Game

To transcend these far-too-common neurotic relationships, I would like to emphasize that effective partnership can provide great opportunities for personal growth. Mature relationships come with lessons to learn and possibilities to evolve. But, of course, the million-dollar question is whether we want to evolve as partners.

Reflecting on the lessons I have learned through listening to my clients, the more successful relationships differ in that the people involved have a greater capacity for commitment. As a couple, the partners are realistic enough not to look for Mr. or Ms. Perfect. Instead, they are more accommodating and have a greater capacity to adapt. They tolerate some imperfections and do not hold on to idealized expectations. Of course, being able to do this necessitates a degree of emotional maturity. It implies having the capacity to negotiate one another's narcissistic needs and knowing how to use one another as an emotional container. This quality of mature dependency means both parties are able to express their feelings about their needs, while creating space for one another.

What differentiates fulfilling partnerships further is the capacity of partners to face existential realities together, the most important of these being aging. Having a good sense of humor can be very helpful, as humor is a highly effective buffer when dealing with the ups-and-downs of daily life. Predictably, such a satisficing relationship is more likely to occur if partners have internalized examples of successful couples.

Let me end by mentioning some specific rules that partners can live by – something that may even be helpful for the recent fairy tale couple. To start with, in any relationship we should be aware of the sirens of lust that can easily lead us astray. Lust plays an important role in love at first sight. When we find ourselves subjected to these rollercoaster emotions, we should try to remain levelheaded enough to consider how our feelings of the past are influencing our present feelings. I realize that this is easier said than done under the influence of a *coup de foudre*. As Federico Garcia Lorca put it, "To burn with desire and keep quiet about it is the greatest punishment we can bring on ourselves." Also, if the decision has been made to embark on a partnership, make it a rule that both parties should be able to express annoyances constructively. It's important not to harp on the negative but to stress the positive. In addition, in relationships, it is not a good idea to see the other as a change project. It's always going to be an uphill struggle to "fix" a partner. If, however, we believe that change is possible, be wise, and start small.

It is important to think about the desirable qualities we want from the other. Reflect on whether the person we are attracted to has the qualities we are looking for, whether that is intelligence, warmth, kindness, honesty, or trustworthiness. We could ask ourselves whether we can be ourselves when together with our partner. And if we are thinking about living together, will each partner be able to accept the good, the bad, and the ugly of the other? Will our partner be able to hang in there when the going gets tough? Last but not least, will we be able to engage in meaningful activities together? People who do so seem to have the most enduring relationships. Having said all this, I can only hope that the new Duke and Duchess of Sussex have taken these rules of engagement to heart and will be happy ever after.

The author O. Henry wrote a famous and very poignant story, *The Gift of the Magi*, which features a perfect partnership. At Christmas, a young married couple want to give each other a gift but they have no money to spare. The wife, however, has beautiful long hair. She decides to sell her hair and use the money to buy a gold chain for her husband's watch. When her husband comes home, he stops short at the sight of her cropped head. The wife explains that she has sold her hair to buy him a present. Her husband has a gift for her as well and hands it to her. It is beautiful combs for her hair. The wife then gives him the watch chain she bought with the money from selling her hair, and her husband explains that he has sold his watch to buy the combs.

24

Why Wisdom Can't Be Taught

The wise man hath his thoughts in his head; the fool, on his tongue.
—Ivan Panin
*To enjoy good health, to bring true happiness to one's family, to bring peace to
all, one must first discipline and control one's own mind. If a man can
control his mind he can find the way to Enlightenment, and all wisdom and
virtue will naturally come to him.*
—Gautama Buddha

The day after he became the CEO of his company, Davis had a dream in which he was walking on a beach and discovered a bottle. He took out the cork and out sprung a genie, who told Davis he could make one wish in exchange for releasing her from her imprisonment. Davis knew exactly what he would wish – not riches, fame, or a long life, but something that would help him in his new position. He was now responsible for the lives of many people, and haunted by doubts that he would be successful in an organization that was going through turbulent times. So, Davis asked for the gift of wisdom, so that he could guide his people in the best way possible.

© The Author(s) 2019
M. F. R. Kets de Vries, *Down the Rabbit Hole of Leadership*,
https://doi.org/10.1007/978-3-319-92462-5_24

This dream probably sounds familiar. It is basically King Solomon's dream, an ageless dream that incorporates a strong moral component. In the Old Testament, God (not a genie) appears before King Solomon and tells him to ask for anything. Solomon asks for "a discerning heart," and God is so pleased with his response that he gives the king both wisdom and riches.

The moral of both these stories is that although Solomon and Davis were in positions of power, they didn't let that go to their head. They made an effort to stay humble, were troubled by their inexperience, and felt unready for the job.

When I was a student at the Harvard Business School, I had to read the classic work by Professor Charles Gragg, "Because Wisdom Can't Be Told." In this article Gragg extolls the virtues of the case method, emphasizing that simply lecturing students about a subject will not ensure that they retain what is being said. However, Gragg was not the first to argue this point. The medical profession has known this for a long time and has always used case studies or war stories as a way to bring future doctors up to speed and help them make wise diagnoses. Millennia earlier, Socrates had the same opinion, saying, "I cannot teach anyone anything, I can only make them think." Unfortunately, while wisdom requires education, education does not necessarily make people wise. As Gragg noted in his article, the mere act of listening to wise statements and sound advice has limited value. It doesn't necessarily lead to wisdom. So are there any ways to expedite the transfer of wisdom? To address this question, we first need to reflect on what wisdom is all about.

What Is Wisdom?

Throughout the ages, philosophers, psychologists, religious leaders, poets, novelists, and people in the helping professions have struggled with what wisdom is. Wisdom seems to be hard to define, but we generally know it when we see it. Some people equate wisdom with intelligence and knowledgeability. But all too often, we see that intelligence and wisdom are quite different things. The world is full of brilliant people who aren't very wise. Instead of showing wisdom, they intellectualize; they do not really understand the essence of things. In contrast, wise people try to grasp the deeper meaning of what is known, but also want to better understand the limits of their knowledge.

There's a great difference between knowing things and knowing how to make use of what we know. Wisdom implies more than merely being able to process information in a logical way. Knowledge only turns into wisdom when we have the ability to assimilate and apply it to make the right (wise) decisions. As the saying goes, knowledge speaks but wisdom listens. Wise people are blessed with good judgment. In addition, they possess the qualities of sincerity and authenticity, the first implying a willingness to say what you mean, the second to be what you are.

Wise people (like King Solomon) are also humble. Their humility derives from a willingness to recognize the limitations of their knowledge. They accept that there are things they will never know. But by accepting their ignorance, they are better prepared to bear their fallibility. People who are wise know when what they are doing makes sense, but also know when it will not be good enough. And ironically, it is exactly this kind of self-knowledge that pushes them to do something about it.

From a conceptual point of view, wisdom can be looked at from both a cognitive and emotional perspective. Cognitively, wise people can see the big picture, put things into perspective, and see things from many points of view (avoiding simplistic black-and-white thinking). They are able to rise above their personal point of view. Emotionally, wise people are reflective, introspective, and tolerant of ambiguity. They know how to manage negative emotions, instead of being the prisoners of such feelings. They have empathy and compassion, qualities that differentiate them in an interpersonal context.

Ironically, what makes wisdom more important than success and riches is that it enables us to live well. In more than one way, wisdom and well-being are close cousins. Wisdom appears to be a positive predictor of successful aging and a longer life. Our mental and physical health flourish when they are congruent with our beliefs and values. As Mahatma Gandhi once said, "Happiness is when what you think, what you say, and what you do are in harmony." Wise people are attuned to what constitutes a meaningful life. They know how to plan for, and manage such a life. This implies self-concordance, behaving consistently with their values, a journey that requires self-exploration, self-knowledge, and self-responsibility.

Wisdom Can't Be Told

So how can we acquire wisdom, which is such a desirable thing to have? Can we expedite its realization? Only through our own experiences (particularly of adversity), will we discover our personal capacity for wisdom, and learn how to create wisdom in our own lives. Becoming wise is an individual quest that no one else can undertake for us, or spare us from. It includes learning how to cope with the major tragedies and dilemmas embedded within our life's journey.

Wise people have pointed out that wisdom dwells in the messiest, most painful of places. Death, illness, aging, and setbacks are life's greatest teachers. Painful as it sounds, setbacks are memorable growth experiences, contributing to a deeper understanding of the vicissitudes of life. Overcoming difficult situations contributes to an increased appreciation of life and the recognition of new possibilities. And it is exactly these kinds of experiences that enable us to rise above our own perspectives – to step out of our selves and see things as they are, not as we are. As Friedrich Nietzsche noted, "That which does not kill us makes us stronger."

Unfortunately, wisdom is not something that automatically comes with age. While older people may be more capable of putting things into perspective (compared to the young), many never put their life experiences to good use. To acquire reflectivity might necessitate the help of others. This is where educators, coaches, psychoanalysts, psychotherapists, and mentors can play a significant role. After all, the ability to discern wisely and make fair judgments and assessments is essential in making these interventions successful.

I believe strongly that people willing to provide guidance should not only disseminate knowledge but also help people searching for wisdom work through challenging experiences – assisting them in making better life choices. Even though we cannot teach wisdom, we can create a foundation that brings wisdom within reach. This means encouraging them to work on emotional awareness, emotional self-regulation, relational skills, and mindfulness. Educators and people in the helping professions need to create the kinds of experiences that enable people who want to continue their self-development to recognize and understand the threads connecting the mental, physical, emotional, spiritual, psychological, and social fabric of their lives. They can guide these people to overcome the inner demons that may have contributed to a sense of being stuck while embarking on these endeavors.

A number of specific steps can be taken to expedite this. For example, in my work with executives I have found that creating a learning community, in which participants have the opportunity to tell their personal stories, has a cathartic effect and also helps wisdom to come to bear. Although structured, written case studies (as Gragg advocated) can be helpful, life case studies narrated by the participants in a learning community have a much more dramatic, emotional impact (I touch on this topic in Chap. 10). Telling and listening to personal stories can be a starting point for a deeper understanding of oneself and others. If people are willing to go through such a process, it will help them become better listeners. They will also learn to hear what's *not* being said.

Participants in these experiential groups can be nudged to play devil's advocate, a role that's essential to the ability to consider other points of view. A learning community is a great context in which to practice open-mindedness. While these exchanges can contribute to a deeper understanding and acceptance of the ambiguous nature of things, people in search of wisdom may also become increasingly aware of the limitations of their knowledge – a key realization in the pursuit of wisdom. And if these experiences are designed in a holistic way, the members of a learning community will be able to integrate knowledge and experiences, gradually becoming more adept at dealing with the challenges that life has to offer.

One essential element of membership of a learning community is encouraging participants to try new things. Searching for novelty can be a great eye-opener. If a safe, transitional space is created within the group, people are more likely to step out of their comfort zone. As part of a group, members learn to deal with people who are very different – individuals they would never otherwise associate with. This can be a very enriching experience. The pressures exerted by the group as a whole may transform the dysfunctional behavior patterns that characterize some of its participants. These group experiences can be great exercises in humility.

Because the life case studies focus on challenges, group participants learn that everyone is fallible. The interactions between the members of the group will encourage them to learn from their mistakes. It may help them to think before acting – to become truly reflective leaders. Finally, participants in this type of experiential learning environment are more likely to take off their masks and live their values more authentically. As they become more aware of their limitations, they may realize that they may need further help in their quest for self-knowledge. They may look for the guidance of wise mentors to provide additional support on their life's journey.

Unfortunately, in our hyperactive digital age, attaining wisdom is becoming a bigger challenge. It has become increasingly difficult to find the time and mental space to make meaningful connections, engage in deep conversations and reflection, and develop emotional awareness, empathy, and compassion. Multi-tasking poses a great challenge when it comes to creating a reflective space. Tablets and mobiles, and all the apps that constantly vie for our immediate attention, are incompatible with the pursuit of wisdom. Within this manic ecosystem, becoming part of a learning community is even more valuable, as wisdom grows in quiet places.

I will end this chapter with an illustration of something that happened in one of these learning communities. An aspiring leader asked a program facilitator what she had learned over the years. What incredible things had made her who she was? She replied that she had always searched for peace of mind. To that end, she had done a lot of reading, had traveled widely, visited many exotic places, seen extraordinary architectural wonders, and been exposed to great displays of power. She had also interacted with many famous people, listened to many great teachers, and read many of their works. But despite all that, nothing gave her more peace of mind than sitting quietly beside a stream, watching the water, and observing the beauty of a sunrise or sunset. As she pointed out to the participant, real living often consists of very simple things.

25

What Next?

We should give meaning to life. Not wait for life to give us meaning.
—Anon.
To live is to suffer, to survive is to find some meaning in the suffering.
—Friedrich Nietzsche

Derek had been a poster boy for executive success. An excellent student at high school, he moved effortlessly to an Ivy League college. During his studies, he met his future wife whom he married soon after graduation. Subsequently, Derek got a position as an associate at a premier strategic consulting firm. Having worked there for a few years, he decided to do an MBA at one of the better-known business schools. After obtaining his degree – financial independence was important to him – he joined one of the major investment banks on Wall Street. With his talent for M&A, Derek became a partner in record time. While climbing the corporate ladder, he had also become the proud father of three daughters.

Derek always seemed very focused, both at work and at home. Although he did not articulate it directly, he saw giving his family a good life by being an excellent provider as life's main purpose. Things changed, however, when his youngest daughter left for college. With the house

© The Author(s) 2019
M. F. R. Kets de Vries, *Down the Rabbit Hole of Leadership*,
https://doi.org/10.1007/978-3-319-92462-5_25

suddenly empty, life took a different turn. He was troubled by feelings of emptiness, and a sense of aimlessness. He wondered what had happened to his past confidence and sense of purpose. Deep down, he felt that he had very little to live for. With his children grown up, the lively and meaningful full-time parenting years were over. It didn't help that, looking back on his life, he realized he had not fully appreciated the time with his children. Work had been too time-consuming. He also felt disconnected from his wife. Generally speaking, having fulfilled his biological destiny, Derek found himself aimless and adrift.

Roots of Human Existence

Like Derek, many of us struggle with questions of meaning in the later stages of life. In the past, our children may have been the focus of attention, but as they leave the home, couples have to take a fresh look at their lives – including their marriage. And they not always like what they see. No wonder that there is a peak in divorce rates when people hit their fifties.[1]

In 1897, Paul Gauguin finished his painting "Where Do We Come From? What Are We? Where Are We Going?" From Gauguin's letters, we know the painting is his meditation on birth, life, and death, using themes from Tahitian mythology. The painting tackles fundamental questions about the roots of human existence, and its meaning. Gauguin considered this painting, done at a time of great personal distress, his masterpiece.

In this context, it is worth reflecting on the comment of the writer Fyodor Dostoyevsky, "The mystery of human existence lies not in just staying alive, but in finding something to live for." In other words, the purpose of life is a life of purpose. Many studies have shown that having a purpose is good for our mental health. If we know why we are here, if we have a reason for our existence, if we have a purpose, we feel more connected and more alive.

Most of us have moments (unbidden or consciously) when we feel we need to account for our existence. We need answers to some fundamental

---

[1] https://www.aarp.org/home-family/friends-family/info-05-2012/life-after-divorce.html

questions: Who am I? Why am I here? What is life all about? What's the meaning of my life? We may even come to the realization that avoiding these existential questions makes life superficial and empty.

A Life Lived Well

From an evolutionary point of view, the answer to these questions is obvious. The primary purpose of life is the continuation of life. A biological program for survival and reproduction underwrites the complex cycles of life, in which death becomes the great equalizer. The primal motivator behind human existence is to pass on our genes to the next generation. Undertaking this evolutionary task brings meaning. But when that task is completed, an existential question emerges: what next?

We could argue that this question haunts us more than ever in this day and age due to the fact that we live much longer, thanks to medical advances. We are not like the Pacific salmon that swim upstream to spawn, only to die immediately afterward. As Derek's example illustrates, human life is far less straightforward. The extension of life expectancy has expanded our existential vacuum. The human imagination struggles to invent new meanings. What can be done to prevent the kind of unexpected malaise people like Derek experience? What can Derek do to feel better?

In his *Nicomachean Ethics*, Aristotle argued that, for optimal well-being, we need to make a distinction between *hedonia* and *eudaimonia*. *Hedonia* relates to subjective needs whose satisfaction leads to momentary pleasure; *eudaimonia*, by contrast, is more objective, and relates to a life lived well. Aristotle maintained that well-being consists of more than transitory pleasures. Our life takes its meaning from the actualization of our potential – living a worthwhile life.

Finding Meaning

As mentioned previously, apart from our biological, evolutionary purpose for living, meaning matters. And meaning refers to understanding who we are, and how we fit into our world.

In the past, people found meaning and comfort in religion. But as the role of religion has decreased in contemporary society, it has become more difficult to find answers to our existential dilemma in religion. But this doesn't mean that we should avoid questioning the meaning of existence.

The psychiatrist and Holocaust survivor Victor Frankl observed, through his own experience in a concentration camp, that those with the greatest chance of survival were not the most physically fit. More important than physical fitness was the strength of a person's belief system. Frankl noted that once a prisoner lost hope for the future, he or she was doomed. It was the ability to find meaning that sustained those that survived. In his book *The Will to Meaning*, Frankl argues that life has no meaning in itself, unless we actively create an existential purpose. Through meaning we can achieve our potential; through meaning we can be the best that we can be. Thus, apart from being steered by our biological imperative, our primary driver in life is not only pleasure in the service of procreation, but the discovery and pursuit of what we personally find meaningful.

Greater purpose in life has been shown to be associated with a number of psychological outcomes, including a more positive outlook on life, greater happiness, more satisfaction, and greater self-esteem. There also seems to be a connection between our psychological state and the ability of our immune system to fight disease. A sense of purpose in life may serve as a buffer against negative health outcomes, especially as we age. For example, people who derive purpose and meaning from daily life, and who work toward specific goals, may function better when aging. As they are highly engaged and focused, and participate in meaningful activities, they will, by extension, have more reasons for living.

Derek is currently experiencing a profound sense of loss, which makes him vulnerable to depression, high levels of anxiety, and more susceptible to substance abuse. He is in the grip of an identity crisis (see Chap. 20), triggered by the change in his family life that has brought to the surface thoughts, fears, and emotions that he has pushed out of conscious awareness for many years.

There are signs that unless he addresses his state of mind, he might be facing a marital crisis. Unless he makes some changes to align his lived and desired experience, between the meaninglessness of everyday life and the desire to find meaning – unless what he thinks, what he says, and what he does, are in harmony – Derek will not be all he could be.

What to Do?

Understanding this, what can we do about Derek's predicament? An existential crisis can permeate every aspect of someone's life and manifest itself in many different ways, including a loss of meaning, a feeling of deep disconnection from the people close to them, or a sense of despair, and the dread of existence. For some, a line of questioning like Gauguin's can lead to depressive reactions, suicidal thoughts, or even suicide attempts. From an existential point of view, Derek's depressive reactions make him more aware of his mortality, but they also challenge him to break out of a self-imposed straitjacket. Derek needs to realize that he is not simply the product of heredity and environment but that he also possesses the ability to make decisions and take responsibility for his own life.

Now that his children have left home, Derek needs to rediscover a sense of worth and purpose. He would do well to reflect on the past, the present, and the future and actively seek out what motivates his inner self. After all, if he doesn't know who he is, he will never know what belongs to him. Looking ahead, he needs to focus on what he loves. He needs to develop knowledge and skills in the service of whatever would make him feel really alive in the long run. He should learn how to balance *eudaimonia* – a life well lived – with *hedonia* by creating happy experiences and moments.

If we are to live a full, rich life, we have no choice but to confront the uncomfortable existential givens that Derek is now grappling with. Although life is everything but a rose garden, the most effective response to an existential crisis is to build caring relationships, seek out empathic listeners, and embark on meaningful pursuits – however small. We need to treasure the simple pleasures of life: walking in nature, admiring a sunset, reading a book, a good conversation, the company of loved ones, and seeing our children grow up.

Here's a Zen story that illustrates how accepting uncomfortable truths can actually bring peace. Once upon a time a peripatetic monk was looking for a place to stay for the night. When it was almost dark, he stopped at an imposing farmhouse, and asked the owner if he could rest there. According to custom, the farmer welcomed him, and treated him as an honored guest. The next morning, when the monk was ready to leave, the farmer asked him if he could give his family his blessing, holding out a scroll for the monk to write on. The monk thought for a moment, then reached for the scroll and wrote: "Father dies, son dies, grandson dies." Then he left. But when he read what the monk had written, the farmer was angry and distressed, and ran after him. "I asked you for a blessing," he cried, "and you have given me a curse." The monk said, "I will rewrite the blessing if you wish. But are you sure? This is the natural order of things. I do not see how things could be otherwise and thought a blessing."

26

The Epitaph Question

I knew if I waited around long enough something like this would happen.
—George Bernard Shaw
The rarest quality in an epitaph is truth.
—Henry David Thoreau

Benjamin Franklin allegedly said, "I wake up every morning at nine and grab for the morning paper. Then I look at the obituary page. If my name is not on it, I get up." What are we to make of this humorous, yet dark comment? At a deeper level it may indicate the way Franklin would like to be remembered. He may have been asking himself what his obituary would look like. Would people remember him positively or negatively?

On the subject of obituaries, it's said that Alfred Nobel made the decision to institute his famous prize after reading about his purported death in a French newspaper that mistook him for his brother, who had died during a visit to Cannes. The article carried the headline, "The Merchant of Death Is Dead."

© The Author(s) 2019
M. F. R. Kets de Vries, *Down the Rabbit Hole of Leadership*,
https://doi.org/10.1007/978-3-319-92462-5_26

Although we all know about the Nobel Prize, we may not know that Nobel's wealth came from the invention of dynamite. To Nobel, the epitaph was a harsh reminder how he would go down in history. No wonder he was horrified. Its severity motivated him to rehabilitate his name: shortly afterward, he changed his will, donating most of his fortune to the Nobel Prize foundation. His memory now lives on, not as a merchant of death, but as an advocate of peace and progress.

So how would you like to be remembered? What would you like to be your epitaph? Thoughts about our legacy influence the trajectory of our life. Consciously or unconsciously, they impact our life choices.

An epitaph is a memorial statement that pays tribute to the deceased, or commemorates a past event. It's usually inscribed on a tombstone or read as part of a funeral oration.

Walking through a graveyard recently I was struck by the generic nature of so many epitaphs: "rest in peace," "always in our thoughts, forever in our hearts," "always together," "a long life well lived." Truly memorable epitaphs were few and far between. I didn't see any to match some of the more famous epitaphs, such as "In" (Jack Lemmon); "Excuse my dust" (Dorothy Parker); "I told you I was ill" (Spike Milligan); "The song is ended, but the melody lingers on" (Irving Berlin); or "She did it the hard way" (Bette Davis).

Early in life, we do not tend to think about our epitaph. But thinking about the sort of obituary or epitaph we would like is something we tend to do as we get older. We begin to realize the importance of living on in the hearts of the people we leave behind.

In my experience, the epitaph question is a very enlightening way to take a long-term perspective on your life and zoom in on what is most important. It pushes you to think about what kind of person you would like to be. By forcing yourself to focus on the big questions, you may obtain greater clarity about what really matters in your life.

Over the years, as part of the various leadership development programs that I run, I have asked many executives what they would like their epitaph to be. This is probably the ultimate exercise in beginning with the end in mind. I ask them what they would like to read on their tombstone. What would they like people to remember them by? And bearing this in mind, what does that indicate may be missing from their life?

Not surprisingly, many executives initially struggle to find an answer to these questions. But they manage after a while, and some of the recurring answers I receive include:

- I'd like to be remembered as a wonderful parent, a thoughtful husband/wife, a caring brother/sister, or friend.
- I'd like people to say that I made a positive difference in their lives – that I was their source of inspiration.
- I'd like to be remembered for standing up for those unable to stand up for themselves.
- I'd like to be remembered as someone who enjoyed life to its fullest – taking each day as a new experience.
- I'd like to be remembered for my sense of humor, my ability to make others laugh and make them feel good.
- I'd like to be remembered as someone that lived life by my own rules, not afraid to take risks – someone able to follow my own path.
- I'd like to be seen as someone whose leadership qualities and successes were driven by compassion, affection, and ambition for others.
- I'd like to be remembered as someone creative and imaginative – who advanced knowledge in my field.
- I'd like to be remembered for my accomplishments and achievements, whether at work or within my community.

What's clear from these comments is that we're not going to be remembered for how much money we earned, our jewelry, the size of our homes, or the type of car we drove. We are going to be remembered for the difference we made in the lives of others. What we do for others is really our enduring legacy. To quote Albert Einstein, "Only a life lived for others is a life worth living." Executives would do well to keep this observation in mind.

To earn a fitting epitaph, you need to be the best version of yourself. This means making a difference in other people's lives. How you want to be remembered is how you ought to live your life. Reflecting now on the kind of epitaph you would like to hear (as Alfred Nobel did), might propel you to make radical changes in your life. Your time is limited, so don't live a meaningless life. Live a life worth remembering.

Here's a story I heard many years ago. An old man was dying, so he asked all his friends and family members – many of whom he hadn't seen for years – to come and say goodbye to him. He had a good word for each of them. He told them he loved them, or that he forgave them, or that he now understood why things had turned out as they had, and that he was at peace with it. For their part, all his visitors had good words to say to him.

While all this was going on, someone who had known the dying man for many years, stood up and said, "We are all fools. We could have said all these things to you years ago. Why didn't we?" Then turning to the dying man, he said, "And why did you bottle all these good feelings up for so long? Why didn't you express them when you were in the prime of your life?"

"I should have done it," said the man, "but happily for me it is not too late to do so now." And he died peacefully.

Bibliography

Bowlby, J. (1988). *A Secure Base* (p. 39). Oxford: Routledge.

Comey, J. (2018). *A Higher Loyalty: Truth, Lies, and Leadership*. New York: Flatiron Books.

Global Research. (2015). *US Wealth Concentration: Wealthiest 10% of America Owns 75% of America.* http://www.globalresearch.ca/u-s-wealth-concentration-wealthiest-tenth-10-of-americans-own-75-of-america/5461246

Kets de Vries, M. F. R. (2012). Star Performers: Paradoxes Wrapped Up in Enigmas. *Organizational Dynamics, 41,* 173–182.

Kets de Vries, M. F. R. (2014). The Psycho-path to Disaster: Coping with SOB Executives. *Organizational Dynamics, 43*(1), 17–26.

Kets de Vries, M. F. R. (2017). *Riding the Leadership Rollercoaster: An Observer's Guide*. London: Palgrave Macmillan.

Mencken, H. L. (Ed.). (1942). *A New Dictionary of Quotations on Historical Principles from Ancient and Modern Sources*. New York: Alfred A. Knopf.

Milgram, S. (1974). *Obedience to Authority: An Experimental View*. New York: Harper Perennial.

© The Author(s) 2019
M. F. R. Kets de Vries, *Down the Rabbit Hole of Leadership*,
https://doi.org/10.1007/978-3-319-92462-5

Pew Research Center. (2015). *American Middle Class Is Losing Ground*. http://www.pewsocialtrends.org/2015/12/09/the-american-middle-class-is-losing-ground/

The Esquire. (2016). *American Rage*. http://www.esquire.com/news-politics/a40693/american-rage-nbc-survey/

Index

© The Author(s) 2019
M. F. R. Kets de Vries, *Down the Rabbit Hole of Leadership*,
https://doi.org/10.1007/978-3-319-92462-5